The Word Received

The Word Received

. . . .

A Homily for Every Sunday of the Year

Year C

William J. Byron, SJ

Paulist Press
New York / Mahwah, NJ

Cover image credits: Red background art by Eky Studio / Shutterstock.com. Yellow
background art by Lucy Baldwin / Shutterstock.com. All rights reserved.
Cover design by Sharyn Banks
Book design by Ericka McCabe

Library of Congress Control Number: 2012950229

ISBN 978-0-8091-4809-7

Published by Paulist Press
997 Macarthur Boulevard
Mahwah, New Jersey 07430

www.paulistpress.com

Printed and bound in the United States of America

Contents

CONTENTS

Dedicated to the memory of
Walter J. Burghardt, SJ
...who taught my generation of American Jesuits
a lot about preaching.

Introduction to Year C

This, like *The Word Proclaimed, Year A,* and *The Word Explained, Year B,* is a book without a theme, unless the liturgical calendar can be said to provide a seasons-of-the-year theme for the Sunday homily. It is, however, a book based on a theory—a theory of the homily—namely, that every homily should be an extension of the proclamation. This is the liturgical principle that underlies every chapter in this book and its two companion volumes that complete the coverage of Years A, B, and C of readings in the Sunday Lectionary.

Sacred Scripture from Old and New Testaments is proclaimed in the first part of every Eucharistic liturgy. The homilist then extends the proclamation by filtering it through his or her own faith experience and tries to match it up with the faith experience of the people in the pews. That is always a challenge; but being mindful of the challenge to extend the proclamation in this way provides the homilist with direction in rendering this service to the people of God. Homilists have a personal responsibility to heed and incorporate into their own style of delivery these words from the pen of St. Augustine: "[I]f I speak to someone without feeling, he does not understand what I am saying" (from a *Treatise on John,* Tract 26).

We are a Sunday people, we Catholic Christians. We gather in Eucharistic assemblies every Sunday to remember the Lord in the breaking of the bread. In this way we give praise and thanks to God. That is our Sunday obligation—to give thanks to God. We thus declare ourselves to be "much obliged"—to be grateful—and we express that gratitude in praise of God and love of neighbor. Gratitude is the foundation of our religious observance. It is in gratitude that we gather to hear the word and share in the breaking of the bread. Nourished every

Sunday by both word and sacrament, we go forth each week to serve our neighbor.

We break open the Scriptures in our Sunday assemblies where we find Christ present not only in (1) the Eucharistic elements, (2) the faithful who are gathered there, and (3) the person of the priest-presider, but also in (4) the proclamation of the word and in the homily. A well-prepared homily is filtered first through the faith experience of the homilist and, so far as possible, matched up to meet the faith experience of the faithful in the pews. Somehow Christ is there in both pulpit and pew.

This book is a collection of one homilist's efforts to extend the proclamation in ways that will touch the hearts and minds of believers. Every chapter in this book is a delivered homily. They've been road-tested in parishes and university chapels. They've been preached, heard, reflected upon, and discussed. Standing alone as a book, apart from any liturgical setting, this collection might prove helpful (if taken just one homily at a time) to the people who belong to any parish community. On the desks of priests and deacons, this book could serve as a source of ideas for extending the proclamation and matching it to the faith experience of those the homilists are privileged to serve.

To the extent that this book proves useful to the occupant of any pulpit or pew, or to any reader interested in reflecting on God's word in quiet moments apart from the crowd, my purpose in putting it together will have been achieved.

I've heard it remarked recently by a disaffected and discouraged Catholic worshipper that in the United States we have "*Saturday Night Live* and Sunday morning dead." I hope this book can help to change that. I've also heard from a pastor who hosted a foreign pastor during a visit to this country that his guest commented to him: "I notice that in your churches the benches and kneelers have cushions; I've noticed that your homilies are usually cushioned too." Perhaps the to-the-point style of the homilies offered here will facilitate the discovery of both challenge and encouragement in the word proclaimed, the word explained, and the word received.

—*W.J.B.*

I
Advent

. . . .

1

First Sunday of Advent

"Your Redemption Is at Hand"

Jeremiah 33:14–16; Psalm 25; 1 Thessalonians 3:12—4:2;
Luke 21:25–28, 34–36

One of my favorite scriptural expressions is a set of words from Psalm 27:14: "Wait for the LORD, take courage; be stouthearted, wait for the LORD!" This is a mantra for me, a breathe-it-in, breathe-it-out rhythmic prayer that I use to hear God speak to me. It is also a Scripture passage that I can use to speak to God. Spoken either to the human heart or from the human heart, these inspired words speak to the human condition: "Wait for the LORD, take courage; be stouthearted, wait for the LORD!" They speak to you, in whatever circumstances you find yourself, any day, every day.

Paul Tillich once wrote: "Our time is a time of waiting; waiting is its special destiny. And every time is a time of waiting, waiting for the breaking in of eternity. All time runs forward. All time, both history and in personal life, is expectation. Time itself is waiting, waiting not for another time, but for that which is eternal."

And so I say to myself, and to you, on this first Sunday of Advent: "Wait for the LORD, take courage; be stouthearted, wait for the LORD!"

Advent. A time of expectancy; a time of patient expectation. A time when, in the words of today's Gospel reading, you should "stand erect and raise your heads because your redemption is at hand." Exercise your imagination right now to "stand erect," on your tiptoes, so to speak, and recognize that your redemption is not only ready but your ransom has already been paid; act however, in this liturgical season and in this imaginative exercise, act as if you are not yet free. Beg for that ransom; yearn for that freedom.

Most of you are free citizens of this nation and, quite probably, you take a moment to celebrate your freedom every July 4. Every one of you is a redeemed and ransomed Christian right now at this very moment, yet your Church invites you to let time stop, if you will, and let your imagination take you back to the time before your redemption, and to let your soul stretch Godward ("To you, O lord, I lift my soul," as today's responsorial psalm puts it) . Put yourself in a prayerful posture where you can indeed "stand erect and raise your heads because your redemption is hand."

What, if anything, does Advent mean for you this year? Are you psychologically able to disconnect momentarily from whatever it is that preoccupies you, to disengage from the fast-paced routine of responsibility at home and at work, from worry and wonder, from fear and fortune, regardless of whether your fortune be good or bad? Can you climb outside your skin for an isolated moment of expectation, anticipation, and faith-based celebration of the thrilling reality that "your redemption is at hand?" Advent asks you to try.

Advent asks you to a acknowledge that there is so much more to the weeks ahead than shopping and wrapping, decorating and donating; so much more than the human warmth, love, and joy that is so much a part of it all. Advent asks you not to let yourself get caught up in the immediacy and materiality of this joyful season. Enjoy it, yes, of course, but use the eye of faith to see through it all quite literally to what is of true and lasting significance, namely, that you are part of a people of God that did indeed "stand erect" and did indeed "raise your heads" to receive a redemption that was then, and is for you now, "at hand."

I think "exciting" is an overworked word in our contemporary vocabulary, but this really is exciting. Your redemption is at hand! Savor the thought. But what if you, for whatever reason, simply cannot savor the thought today? You may be feeling flat and dry; you may be not quite ready to get your expectation mechanism cranked up and running. There may be a restlessness and discontent within; you may be out of focus. Give yourself some time; let Advent work its charm on you.

Your restlessness within may enable you to say with St. Augustine, "You have made us for yourself, O Lord, and our hearts are restless until they rest in you." That is certainly a familiar part of the human condition, and a familiar prayer for many modern Christians. And if those words do speak to you, you may find yourself helped by less well known words of Augustine, from his *Confessions*, words from the fifth century that speak well, I think, to twenty-first-century Christian hearts. Yours may be one of them:

> Late have I loved you, O Beauty so ancient and so new; late have I loved you. For behold you were within me, and I outside; and I sought you outside and in my unloveliness fell upon those lovely things that you have made. You were with me, and I was not with you. I was kept from you by those things, yet had they not been in you, they would not have been at all. You called and cried to me to break open my deafness and you sent forth your beams and you shone upon me and chased away my blindness. You breathed fragrance upon me, and I drew in my breath and do now pant for you. I tasted you, and now hunger and thirst for you. You touched me, and I have burned for your peace.

That is a special form of Advent expectancy. Yours and mine may be less poetic and less palpable. Your Advent expectancy and mine may be a simple faith-based conviction that we are now invited to "Wait for the LORD, take courage; be stouthearted, wait for the LORD!"

2

Second Sunday of Advent

The Things That Really Matter

Baruch 5:1–9; Psalm 126; Philippians 1:4–6, 8–11; Luke 3:1–6

"And this is my prayer: that your love may increase ever more and more in knowledge and every kind of perception, to discern what is of value, so that you may be pure and blameless for the day of Christ..." (Phil 1:9–10)

Let me focus on just one phrase from this morning's readings on this the Second Sunday of Advent; just one phrase from Paul's letter to the Philippians. You heard this simple phrase a moment ago: that you may "discern what is of value."

Paul offers encouragement and advice to the Christian people of Philippi and expresses his hopes for them with these words, that you "may discern what is of value, so that you may be pure and blameless for the day of Christ."

Today I bring those same words forward through the centuries and say to you in your Advent expectancy that you should try to value the things that really matter, up to the very day of *Christmas*. I substituted *Christmas* for *Christ*, you no doubt noticed, and I did so by way of wanting to suggest that there is an Advent strategy that you might employ to try to focus in these weeks before Christmas on "what is of value." Make a special Advent effort to learn to value the things that really matter.

Interesting, isn't it, that those two words "value" and "matter" are packaged together in the one phrase I just used. If your values are right, you'll manage "matter" quite well. You won't get caught in the trap of materialism. Spirit and matter will have a proper balance in your life.

Learn to value the things that really matter. If *Newsweek* (December 11, 2000) is to be believed, "American shoppers are saying 'charge it' 2 million times per hour during this holiday season. By Christmas Day, they'll have added $100 billion to their credit card balances." That's a lot of material and, presumably, a lot of that really matters to American shoppers.

Does it tell us anything about their values? Not necessarily. Material things are important; we can't get along without them. The question, of course, is: to what extent have we become addicted to material things? To what extent are we materialistic? To what extent have we permitted material values to outweigh immaterial values like love, knowledge, caring and concern for others in our lives?

Just because you happen to be running up credit card expenses at this time of year, that, of itself, is no evidence that you are materialistic, that you are addicted to material things. It simply says you are buying, presumably with the intention of giving, material things. It could indeed be saying that you are generous, and generosity, of course, is an immaterial, spiritual value. So go back to the lesson we are focusing on in the section we heard today from Paul's Letter to the Philippians: "Discern what is of value."

I doubt that anyone here fits Oscar Wilde's definition of a cynic: a person "who knows the price of everything and the value of nothing." You may have a pretty good eye for prices, but that is no indication that you have no eye at all for the things that really matter.

A value is something that you cherish, hold dear. What you value, you judge to be worth your time and an appropriate portion of your treasure. Upon reflection, you will probably notice that what you really value, the persons and things that really matter in your life, are quite literally priceless; they cannot be bought and sold.

Notice how the word *value* relates to other words like *valid, valor,* and *valence.* Valence has to do with weight, as every chemistry student knows. What is it that carries the weight in your life, in your value system? Valor is a noble quality; it relates to courage. What do you courageously cherish in life; what is it for which you would put your treasure, yourself, even your life on the line? Valid means founded on truth, having legal recognition, capable of being justified. Are your possessions and relationships valid? Is what you cherish justifiable?

Can your heart rest comfortably where your treasure is because both—your heart and your treasure—are rooted in truth?

Learn to value the things that really matter "up to the very day of Christ," or, as I have reverently altered that line earlier, "up to the very day of *Christmas*." Take a moment or two today to jot down a list of your values, the persons and things that you treasure, cherish, hold dear, that you consider to be worthy of your time and treasure. Write down, if you will, a list under this heading: "My Values." And then take another few moments to fill in this sentence: "I subscribe to [fill-in-the-blank] values." For example, I subscribe to Catholic values, Ignatian values; or, if you are honest with yourself and you notice that other sets of values are more prominent in your life, you might find yourself saying, I subscribe to Democratic values, Republican values, Libertarian values, individualistic values, secular values, humanistic values. You be the judge. Just be an honest judge (always difficult in your own case) and make an honest effort to list those personal values and those systems of values that influence your life.

Once listed, examine them. How do they line up against the simple instruction we've been considering this morning from Philippians: "Discern what is of value"?

Happy pondering, happy discerning for the rest of Advent!

3

Third Sunday of Advent

In Petitions Full of Gratitude

Zephaniah 3:14–18a; Isaiah 12; Philippians 4:4–7; Luke 3:10–18

There are a lot of lively, bouncy, joyful words in today's Scripture readings, your readings for this Third Sunday in Advent known universally as Gaudete Sunday. It is a day of rejoicing, a day of happiness.

"Shout for joy, O daughter Zion," commands the prophet Zephaniah, "sing joyfully, O Israel!" He continues, "Be glad and exalt with all your heart."

Are you in the mood for this? I hope so, because the same urging is expressed in the responsorial verse taken from the prophet Jeremiah: "Cry out with joy and gladness: for among you is the great and Holy One of Israel."

The second reading, from Paul to the Philippians, literally bursts out with the words, "Rejoice in the Lord always. I shall say it again: rejoice!" Paul goes on to offer you the instruction: "Have no anxiety at all, but in everything, by prayer and petition, with thanksgiving, make your requests known to God." I'm going to pick up on that note of gratitude for the theme of this homily: you are to do this "with thanksgiving." But first let me underscore the message proclaimed by John the Baptist in today's Gospel reading. John, St. Luke tells you, "preached good news to the people." And what was that good news? That the fellow with two coats should give one to the poor. That those with food should give to the hungry. That tax collectors should be fair. That soldiers should not bully and should be content with their pay. And that one was coming, the Christ, whose sandal strap John was not fit to loosen, who was greater than John in every way, and who would gather the faithful, like wheat, into his granary.

Good reason to be joyful, to be grateful. Good words to lift our spirits as we pass the mid-point of Advent and prepare ourselves to celebrate Christmas. We have lots on our minds related to the coming celebration of Christmas. Some are preoccupied with what to give; some are dreaming about what might be received. All are behind schedule and unprepared. Most are excited and trying to be happy. 'Tis the season to be jolly, whether or not deep down, inside your skin and within your heart, you may be anything but jolly. Which is not to say that you cannot be grateful. Give gratitude a try as part of your Advent preparation.

You should be presenting your needs to God in prayer and in petitions full of gratitude. Good Advent advice. We all have petitions, some related directly to Christmas, but can we honestly say we are placing our petitions with hearts full of gratitude?

Gratitude is a prototypically Catholic characteristic and is, in my view, central to our Catholic identity.

Consider this question: How would you reduce our Catholic religion to one word? How would you describe who and what we are as Catholics, if you were restricted to a one-word response?

I've said it often and would argue the point anytime, that if I were pressed to reduce the entire meaning of religion to one word, that word would be gratitude. The case for making that one word "love" instead of "gratitude" is worth attempting, but I recall learning from the First Letter of John that it was God who first loved us, thus enabling us to love by his good gift of love and therefore all we can be is grateful. Why? Because he first loved us; he graced us. "In this is love: not that we have loved God, but that he [first] loved us and sent his Son as expiation for our sins" (1 Jn 4:10).

I am also fond of reminding anyone who cares to listen that the old American vernacular used to express gratitude by simply saying, "Much obliged." Obligation under God springs from a sense of gratitude. Acknowledge gratitude as your only stance before God, and you begin to notice the presence of moral obligation to do or not do certain things that God wants you to do or avoid.

There is a multiplier effect associated with gratitude, and the wonder of it all is that gratitude can, if you let it stretch your mind, magnify your happiness.

Are you a grateful, giving person? The closer you get to open and generous sharing, the clearer the signal you are sending to others that gratitude is driving your decisions.

There are stages in your degree of growth in gratitude, in showing yourself to be "much obliged." Where are you now? The higher you rise in your sense of gratitude, the closer you are to genuine holiness.

Count your blessings and be thankful. St. Ignatius of Loyola, founder of the Jesuit Order, once remarked that he saw ingratitude as the root of all sinfulness. A contemporary Jesuit told me recently that he is convinced that a grateful person cannot also be sad. His point is that gratitude and unhappiness cannot coexist in the same person at the same time. So, if you are unhappy, take a moment to check on your gratitude quotient. You may be suffering from a serious gratitude deficit that will, upon examination, explain your unhappiness.

So it is important to think about gratitude, even pray about it. This is a recommended Advent exercise. Let me urge you to review the past twelve months. You should be able to find a lot of gratitude prompters there—first, gratitude for the gift of life and many graces, and for the foundational gift of faith. Then continue down the list of the many reasons you have to be grateful. This is a healthy exercise at any time, but particularly appropriate for Advent.

Being Catholic means always living in gratitude for all of God's gifts. We Catholics present ourselves as "much obliged" (grateful) before God every Sunday. In Advent, we prepare ourselves in joy to welcome Christ at Christmas by letting our minds and hearts dwell on the gratitude that has a home there all year round.

4

Fourth Sunday of Advent

Mary's Greatest Virtue

Micah 5:1–4a; Psalm 80; Hebrews 10:5–10; Luke 1:39–45

This Gospel story of the Visitation—Mary's visit, out of consideration and concern, to her pregnant cousin Elizabeth—provides a clue to what was, without doubt, Mary's greatest virtue—her faith.

Did you notice a tribute to the faith of Mary in Elizabeth's words? "For at the moment the sound of your greeting reached my ears," said Elizabeth to Mary, "the infant in my womb leaped for joy." (That infant, as you know, was John the Baptist.) Elizabeth immediately adds: "Blessed are you [Mary] who believed that what was spoken to you by the Lord would be fulfilled." What was spoken? She's referring to the words that the Angel Gabriel delivered, disclosing to Mary that she would become the Mother of God. "How can this be?," asked Mary at the moment of the Annunciation. And Gabriel explained to her how the Holy Spirit would come upon her and by the power of the Spirit, she would conceive. And Mary then said, "May it be done to me according to your word." She trusted. She conceived.

Blessed is she who trusted, Elizabeth is saying. Blessed is Mary among all women, says Elizabeth, because she believed. And because she believed, because she consented to God's plan as disclosed to her by Gabriel, she conceived the infant that Elizabeth referred to as "the fruit of your womb."

It is a healthy Advent exercise to sort out what I like to think of as the "imitable" versus the "in-imitable" virtues and honors of Mary. So many of the in-imitable ones are there in art and architecture—Virgin Birth, Mother of God, Queen of Heaven, Annunciation, Immaculate Conception, Assumption. They celebrate the uniqueness of Mary; they are her titles to admiration and glory.

Her "imitable" virtues, on the other hand, are often overlooked and underappreciated. Chief among these is her faith. Others would be her tact (remember the marriage feast at Cana?), her courage (recall the flight into Egypt?), her fidelity to Joseph, and her gentle compassion for other people. They are all clearly imitable. But think about her faith. What a pity that we do not focus more on her great and always imitable virtue of faith. What a loss that we do not make a point of imitating her faith in a world so much in need of faith.

Our Lady of Mercy—fine. Our Mother of Consolation—beautiful. Our Mother of Sorrows—comforting. Our Mother of Good Counsel—wonderful. Our Lady of Lourdes—yes, indeed. But why not "Our Lady of Faith"? Why do we not consciously associate faith with Mary? Why over the centuries, right up to the present day, have we been missing an opportunity for devotional reassurance and practical imitation that would enrich our spiritual lives by *seeing* faith whenever we see Mary, and *living* faithfully in imitation of her? We can and should be *doing* faith daily in imitation of this woman of faith who is also our Blessed Mother!

Faith is the act by which we entrust ourselves to God. Who has ever done that better than Mary? Faith is God's gift to us. Who was ever more gifted, more faith-filled than Mary? Devotion to and imitation of Our Lady of Faith will surely make us better disciples of Jesus because Mary was, in fact, the first disciple!

We tend to want to put Mary on a pedestal and that is understandable. But we should beware of putting Mary out of reach. Her faith puts her definitely within our reach. What better way to honor her than by imitating her faith and faithfulness?

Through the centuries, Mary has been proposed to admiring young Catholics as a model of modesty and chastity. No one could argue against our need today for good examples and inspiration along those lines. But even there, there is a need for the young to have faith in themselves as well as faith in God if they are to be modest and remain chaste. Practice of Mary-like faith is recommended to all who want to honor and imitate Mary, the Mother of God.

Blessed is she who trusted that the Lord's words to her would be fulfilled. Let this Advent reflection deepen your conviction that you, too, are blessed because you have trusted and continue to trust that the Lord's words to you will be fulfilled.

II
Christmas Season

. . . .

5

Christmas Vigil

Forever I Will Sing the Goodness of the Lord

Isaiah 62:1–5; Psalm 89; Acts 13:16–17, 22–25; Matthew 1:1–25

This is the Christmas Vigil; not yet Midnight, not yet Christmas Day, but the Vigil of Christmas. The readings are both anticipatory and celebratory. The first reading—from Isaiah—just says flat out "I will not be silent," "I will not be quiet." And Isaiah goes on to assure you that "the LORD delights in you." Indeed he does, so sing we must! We have a Savior. We are thrilled; we are grateful.

The responsorial psalm put the following words on our lips: "For ever I will sing the goodness of the Lord." Forever? Yes. Now that doesn't mean we should be singing endlessly now, while still on this earth, but it does mean that an endless day awaits us, eternal awareness will be ours, and eternal life will be a song of celebration of the goodness of the Lord.

In the Divine Office, the breviary, the hymn for Morning Prayer on Thursday of Week III puts it this way: "In heav'n our joy will be / to sing eternally: /May Jesus Christ be praised. / May earth and sea and sky / From depth to height reply: / May Jesus Christ be praised."

Now, I have to confess that more than once I've wondered, as I've read those words in the breviary, whether I would consider it a genuine joy to "sing eternally." I'd like to talk; there will be countless others available for long and interesting conversations! I think I'd like to read—there is so much I've not gotten around to reading on this book-strewn earth! But singing? I don't think so. That's not mine to decide, however; I'll be happy to do as I am told!

The point of this liturgy, of course, is to focus on the "goodness of the Lord," whose goodness decreed from all eternity that the Second Person of our Triune God would be born—take flesh—in the humble circumstances we recall at this hour, that he would live among us in

19

order to instruct us on the essentials of the good life, and then move through death on a cross into resurrected glory so that we too can live with him forever. "Forever I will sing the goodness of the Lord." What a gift! Who could ask for more?

You will be exchanging gifts soon. That's a wonderful Christmas custom. The gifts we exchange are little more than trinkets when compared to the gift each of us has received in the person of Jesus Christ and in all that he did for us. So celebrate we must tonight and what we are celebrating is the "goodness of the Lord."

And unworthy as we may regard ourselves to be at this moment; as tired, frustrated and unfulfilled as we may considers ourselves to be, we simply must listen to Isaiah and believe him when he says, "The Lord delights in you." If God delights in you, as he most surely does, how can you not delight in yourself at Christmas—the special day on which we recall and give thanks for the coming of the One who gave himself for us and lives within us, and in whom—you and Christ within you—your God takes special delight.

At the funeral in 2011 of Peter F. O'Malley, a well-known Washington, DC-area lawyer who was active in Maryland politics, a generous philanthropist, and a loyal board member at his alma mater Mount St. Mary's University, a story was told that relates to the Christmas Vigil some years ago. Peter had dropped in to see his pastor at St. Louis Parish in Clarksville, Maryland early that afternoon, and while he was there, a homeless man came by seeking assistance. The pastor responded to that request and then Peter took the man aside and asked if he had any plans for dinner that evening, Christmas Eve. Not surprisingly, he didn't, so Peter said "I'll be back here for the 4:00 p.m. Mass—the Christmas Vigil—and I'll look for you here. After Mass, I'll take you home with me for Christmas Eve dinner."

That was just one way in which Peter O'Malley, walked the walk of Christianity and followed in the footsteps of Christ. It was Peter's way of singing the "goodness of the Lord" in the spirit of Christmas love.

Regrettably, I'm told, the man did not return to take Peter up on his invitation. But the invitation was extended and it was sincere. It said something about Christmas to the man who received it; it said a lot about Christmas in the heart of the man who issued it.

6

Christmas Mass During the Night

Christmas Light and Darkness

Isaiah 9:1–6; Psalm 96; Titus 2:11–14; Luke 2:1–14

You heard some stirring words from the great prophet Isaiah in the first reading. Those words ring out in song and solemn proclamation all across the Christian world tonight. "The people who walked in darkness have seen a great light; upon those who dwelt in the land of gloom a light has shone" (Is 9:1).

Regrettably, centuries after these words of Isaiah were spoken we moderns , can, in a certain sense, regard ourselves as fellow travelers with Isaiah's people who "walked in darkness" and "dwelt in a land of gloom." The human condition, we might be tempted to say, has not changed all that much over twenty centuries of war, and want, and selfish disregard for the rights and needs of others. But we know that the birth of Christ has changed the human condition, even though we must admit that the supporting evidence for this assertion of Christmas faith is sometimes hard to find. All the more reason, then, for us to reflect anew tonight on the power of Christmas—a power that disperses darkness and gloom. We have to reflect on the power of Christmas if we are going to maintain perspective, keep our balance, and remain hopeful in our own age of ambiguity.

Isaiah spoke of a "people who walked in darkness." His phrase is fairly descriptive of humanity without Christ, who is, of course, the Light of the World. The prophet described those people as "dwelling in a land of gloom." Christian tradition has repeated these prophetic phrases down through the ages for the precise purpose of celebrating the dispersal of darkness and the lifting of gloom by the coming of Christ, who is forever—this night and every night and day—our light and joy. And yet, for many, perhaps even for some of us, the reality of darkness and gloom persists within us and around us so that the

21

Christmas celebration might have a hollow ring; it can be somewhat forced and unconvincing, a day to be endured rather than enjoyed. Not for all, of course, but for some. And we have to be concerned because those some are a precious part of us.

Every Christmas is celebrated in an "Anno Domini," a "Year of Our Lord." Try to recall how as the Year of Our Lord 2000, also known as Y2K, was about to open up for us, remember how apprehensive we were and conscious of our technological dependency on the computer. We made it over that hurdle nicely, didn't we? We may have forgotten then, as we could easily forget now, to ask ourselves: How can the Lord's year, any year, be a year of gloom? Jesus is Lord, but never a Lord of gloom! Quite the opposite. Under his lordship, gloom is destroyed forever and a joyous peace is available to all who believe in Christ. Perhaps that gloom—undeniably present in many human hearts in different circumstances, places, and periods of history—is a measure of our distance, as a people, from Christ. To be a dweller in the land of gloom is to refuse somehow submission to his loving lordship. That submission, as we who struggle to meet the demands of discipleship know, is never easy.

Sad to say, on any Christmas you can look around and see suffering and death, disease and decay, violence and fear, hatred and injury. You can see broken promises and smashed hopes. But you also see around you goodness and love, generosity and trust, service and life, hope and faith. You see covenants kept and you see fidelity in all its forms at work to keep the human community moving forward on a course of justice.

Modern men and women have cause to claim a peace that is not complacent, a joy that is not naive. To the extent that this is explainable, the explanation lies in the power of Christmas. To the extent that this is visible, the visibility lies in human kindness shown to others, one by one, during the course of any day, not just Christmas Day.

Power in any circumstance is the ability to cause or prevent change. God's power has changed us. The whole human race once walked in darkness; we now have access to the light. But we humans also have power. Each one of us is powerful enough to resist the change from darkness to light. Not just to resist in a superficial way by preferring to nurse our grudges, refusing to forgive, or wallowing in self-pity, but in the profound and tragic form of resistance mentioned early in the Gospel of John (typically proclaimed at Masses "during the day" on Christmas): "And this is the verdict, that the light came into the world, but people preferred darkness to light, because their works were evil." When a human person is powerful with a power that is not of God, he or she condemns himself or herself to walk in darkness. But when empowered by faith and divine love—as you my friends, all of you are, I pray, empowered tonight—then the human person can disperse the darkness and lift the gloom.

The power that generates the darkness of violence and hatred, of greed and grinding fears, often resides in institutions—in the ways we have of doing things. In any society there are institutional arrangements that contain but do not harness power—institutional arrangements that fail to reflect the goodness of persons in their midst. The goodness is there, in you. The kindness is there, in you. Human kindness is a revelation of the divine. God is there—in you, in your midst. And you can change those institutional arrangements!

Christmas lights on trees and roofs, and in the windows of our homes, communicate warmth and welcome to the beholder. But the Christmas light in the features of your face, in the face of the believer, says so much more. It repeats the message of Paul to Titus: "For the grace of God has appeared, saving all and training us to reject godless ways and worldly desires and to live temperately, justly, and devoutly in this age..." (Titus 2:11–12). The offer is irrevocable, the offer of light, the offer of salvation that Christmas brings.

As a wise and witty priest I once knew liked to describe this irrevocable offer, "Jesus promises you two things, and it's a standing promise: Your life will have meaning, and you're going to live forever. If you can find a better offer, take it!" You'll never get a better offer. Now that "the grace of God has appeared," you need not walk in darkness; you will never have to dwell in the land of gloom.

The good news of salvation, the familiar Gospel message in the reading from Luke tonight, is *readable* in the New Testament. It is *audible* wherever the Gospel story of Christ's birth is proclaimed or sung. And it is intended by God to be *visible* in the life of the believer—in you. This is the power of Christmas. This is light in our world today.

For us, the darkness has ended; the land of gloom has been left behind. What St. Paul wrote centuries ago to the Ephesians, remains true for us today:

> For you were once darkness, but now you are light in the Lord. Live as children of light, for light produces every kind of goodness and righteousness and truth. Try to learn what is pleasing to the Lord. Take no part in the fruitless works of darkness; rather expose them, for it is shameful even to mention the things done by them in secret; but everything exposed by the light becomes visible, for everything that becomes visible is light. Therefore, it says: "Awake, O sleeper, and arise from the dead, and Christ will give you light" (Eph 5:8–14).

A blessed Christmas to you all!

7

Christmas Mass at Dawn

"Let Us Go Then to Bethlehem"

Isaiah 62:11–12; Psalm 97; Titus 3:4–7; Luke 2:15–20

We can all say with the angels on this early Christmas morning, "Let us go, then, to Bethlehem to see this thing that has taken place, which the Lord has made known to us."

This is exactly what St. Ignatius of Loyola would have you do if you were making his *Spiritual Exercises,* the famous collection of mediations and contemplations that he put together centuries ago into a handbook to guide a person through a spiritual retreat intended to assist that person in gaining an understanding of and commitment to the will of God for him or her.

Ignatian spirituality is a Christocentric spirituality; so it is no surprise that Ignatius approached the mystery of the birth of Christ with special interest, reverence, and enthusiasm. He would have you—the retreatant, the person making the Exercises—approach this mystery with reverence and enthusiasm too. Ignatius was big on engaging the imagination in personal prayer. He would have the person at prayer make what is called a "composition of place." This means visualizing the scene, if that is possible, and it always is possible when your prayer is based on a scene from the Gospels. You read that Scripture passage and then compose yourself in place and you "re-construct" the event as you find it in Scripture. In the case of the birth of Christ, you picture the stable or cave, you see (and even smell) the animals, the straw, the manger. You welcome the shepherds and you squeeze in with them, make a place for yourself beside them and see the scene through their eyes, exactly as they saw it.

Here is how Ignatius explains what he has in mind here. In the so-called "first point" for your mediation on the birth of Jesus, Ignatius writes: "This will consist in seeing the persons, namely Our Lady, St.

Joseph, the maid, and the Child Jesus after his birth. I will make myself a poor little unworthy slave," says Ignatius, "and as though present, look upon them, contemplate them, and serve them in their needs with all possible homage and reverence. Then I will reflect on myself that I may reap some fruit" (*Spiritual Exercises*, 113).

The words "and serve them in their needs" are taken by some commentators to establish a point of origin in Ignatian spirituality of the notion of service—whole-hearted service—as a characteristic of Ignatian spirituality.

So let yourself "go over to Bethlehem" right now, this morning; let yourself become part of the scene. Let your imagination run. Hear what is being said. This is the first Christmas; it is happening right now around you. "Look upon them," says Ignatius; "contemplate them, and serve them in their needs with all possible homage and reverence." Integrate this notion of service into your contemporary understanding of the meaning of Christmas. If that integration works, service will become part of your Christmas observance, of your Christmas celebration. Christmas without service will no longer be Christmas for you!

What a revolution that would be, if all who celebrate Christmas did so not simply in the exchange of gifts, and in song, and in sharing food and drink together, but celebrated Christmas in service one to another! The shepherds may have rendered some simple service when they went over to Bethlehem. We don't know. The Gospel story simply says, "So they went in haste and found Mary and Joseph, and the infant lying in the manger. When they saw this, they made known the message that had been told them about this child. All who heard it were amazed by what had been told them by the shepherds."

Recall that Ignatius advised anyone contemplating this Nativity scene to be quiet in the face of the mystery and, in his words, "Then I will reflect on myself that I may reap some fruit."

What fruit can you derive from this reflection? I cannot prescribe or predict what you will draw from your personal and private reflection. I can only urge you on this Christmas morning to become part of the scene. Be reflective in front of the manger. And let the Lord of Lords and King of Kings there before you in speechless infancy, speak to your heart. He will speak; all you can do is listen.

May Christmas peace be forever yours.

8

Christmas Mass During the Day

Behind the Christmas Event

Isaiah 52:7–10; Psalm 98; Hebrews 1:1–6; John 1:1–18

Christmas peace! May abundant Christmas grace and joy be yours this morning.

The readings that the Church offers for your reflection in this third of our Christmas Masses celebrating the Nativity of the Lord, the readings of this "Mass During the Day," as it is called, are beautifully theological—mystical really—somewhat above or removed from the flesh-and-blood, straw-and-animal, manger-and-chill, Madonna-and-Child picture that you carry in your imagination: Mary, Joseph, and the Child, in a stable, surrounded by shepherds, as it is represented here at the front of the church in our Christmas crib. The message in this morning's readings invites you to close your eyes and move, as it were, through the proscenium of this manger scene to contemplate the reality of the awesome power of God that hovers above it all.

Reflect for a moment on the power of God at work in this event. Separate the event for a moment, if you can, from the mystery behind it and above it, in order to grasp, however incompletely, some understanding of God's eternal word, some measure of God's powerful love that lies hidden behind the Christmas event.

Forgive me, if you must, for being theological in this homily; thank me, if you will, for not being sentimental in talking about Christmas. I certainly do not want to be academic in these comments, but I do want to help you move through the tangible trappings to an appreciation and better understanding of the triumph of faith that awaits you in the contemplation of the scene of our Lord's Nativity.

Listen to one of the very early Church Fathers, St. Hippolytus, who wrote many centuries ago:

God was all alone and nothing existed but himself when he determined to create the world. He thought of it, willed it, spoke the word and so made it...Apart from God there was simply nothing else. Yet although he was alone, he was manifold because he lacked neither reason, wisdom, power, nor counsel. All things were in him and he himself was all. At a moment of his own choosing and in a manner determined by himself, God manifested his Word [note that theologians explain this word to be not simply an external utterance, but the efficacious self-communication of God to the world; the word contains the power and dynamism of God's creative function] and through him [the Word] he made the whole universe.

Hippolytus continues:

When the Word was hidden within God himself, he was invisible to the created world, but God made him visible. First God gave utterance to his voice, engendering light from light, and then he sent his own mind into the world as its Lord. Visible before to God alone and not to the world, God made him visible so that the world could be saved by seeing him. This mind that entered our world was made known as the Son of God. All things came into being through him; but he alone is begotten by the Father.

Beautiful. Profound. Worthy of reflection.

We bow before the manger in order that our mind's eye might move through the scene to behold the saving power that hovers over it. "God sent his own mind into the world" in this Christmas event!

Remember that, as you ponder the words you just heart in the Gospel reading. They are familiar words from the prologue to the Gospel of John: "In the beginning was the Word, and the Word was with God, and the Word was God. He was in the beginning with God. All things came to be through him, and without him nothing came to be. What came to be through him was life, and this life was the light of the human race; the light shines in the darkness, and the darkness has not overcome it."

Nor, you can safely say, will the darkness of evil and sin, of terrorism and war, of hatred and injustice ever overcome it. Nor will the darkness of doubt that some of us have to deal with, nor the illnesses we bear, nor the reversals and disappointments that tend to get us down ever overcome us, so long as we turn to and remain close to the Light of the World.

"The true light," writes St. John in the words you heard proclaimed today, "The true light, which enlightens everyone, was coming into the world." That's what we see in this manger scene. "He was in the world, and the world came to be through him, but the world did not know him. He came to what was his own, but his own people did not accept him. But to those who did accept him [and that, dear friends, is a reference to every one of you!] he gave power to become children of God, to those who believe in his name [another reference to you!], who were born not by natural generation nor by human choice nor by a man's decision but of God [a reference to your rebirth in baptism!]."

Then John gives the pronouncement that brings us to our knees in grateful adoration: "And the Word became flesh and made his dwelling among us, and we saw his glory, the glory as of the Father's only Son, full of grace and truth."

There is so much there to contemplate. There is so much cause for wonder. There is so much reason to be grateful. And there is so much hope waiting to work its way deeper into your heart, if only you will let the key of faith open your heart to receive it. No matter how bad things appear to be around you, no matter how little faith you have in yourself, no matter how frightened you are, no matter how guilty you feel, no matter how empty you may be today, fall on your knees before the mystery and majesty of Christmas and let this Infant do for you what he was born to do for all, namely, rescue you from the darkness, bring you into the light, save you from your sins, and offer you the promise of eternal life. Merry Christmas!

9

Feast of the Holy Family, Sunday in the Octave of Christmas

Reflections on Faith and Family

1 Samuel 1:20–22, 24–28; Psalm 84; Colossians 3:12–13;
Luke 2:41–52

The famous opening sentence in Tolstoy's *Anna Karenina* always runs through my mind on this Feast of the Holy Family: "All happy families are alike but an unhappy family is unhappy after its own fashion." Christmastime is as close as we ever come to having all families happy. Why are highways, and air and rail terminals crowded at this time of year? Where is everyone going? Home to family and friends, for the most part; or off for a holiday break after spending some time with family. Generous and thoughtful efforts bordering on rescue operations take place in every community to "make sure" that isolated, unrelated persons living alone have "a place to go" for Christmas dinner. The place to go is family, someone's family at any rate. Those who are fond of compiling "happiness is" lists would surely agree that "sadness is" dining alone on Christmas Day.

Unhappy families, each after its own fashion, are part of the Christmas season reality. The big day ends badly in many households. The probability of change or improvement in the New Year is often not high.

The Church speaks to families—happy and unhappy—on this Sunday between Christmas and New Year's Day. It is the Feast of the Holy Family, honoring Jesus, Mary, and Joseph as a family unit worthy of imitation. Familiar Scripture readings of enduring beauty are proclaimed on this day. They are extended into homilies and listened to with faith. The readings do not change but the social forces surrounding family life do change, so much so that it has become necessary for the good of family and society alike to bring faith and family together for reflective purposes in the Christmas season.

This means returning to the fundamental meaning of family, the social unit that draws life from the love of a man for a woman and a woman for a man, a social unit that fosters the attitudes of care and concern, where mature adults are called to a vocation of service to life, and to live that vocation by laying down their lives, day by day, for one another and for the children their love brings forth.

It is a commonplace that cannot be repeated too often that the family is the cornerstone of society. It is our fundamental, foundational social unit. Where family life is in trouble, society is also in trouble, deep trouble. Many of the troubles in contemporary American society derive directly from the troubles in American family life. And where something goes deeply and disastrously wrong in the family, it is usually because members of the family refuse to measure up to the demands of sacrifice.

The word *sacrifice* means "to make holy." No family can be a "holy family" without sacrifices. And no family can be a happy family unless they rest on holiness—not pietistic, multiple-devotion "holiness," but genuine holiness—sacrifice that requires the gift of self to and for others.

Not that many decades ago, before the Catholic Mass changed from Latin to the vernacular, the Wedding Mass in the United States began with an English "exhortation" read by the priest to the couple about to exchange their vows. It contained a great deal of wisdom capable of holding families and societies together. The heart of that exhortation is expressed in these few words: "Let the security of your wedded life rest on the great principle of self-sacrifice. Sacrifice is usually difficult and irksome: only love can make it easy and perfect love can make it a joy." Love, in the wisdom vocabulary of the Church, is another word for sacrifice.

The absence of sacrifice in our homes and in our nation explains, to no small extent, the absence of familial and national happiness.

Something happened to America after World War II. "Affluence" is one way of describing it. Our present national discontent and unease invite us to face up to the fact that sparing and sharing will be more beneficial than the unimpeded consumerism and waste to which we've grown accustomed over the past few decades. In our families, we've seen disturbing divorce rates, deeper loneliness, and much alienation; this is evidence that the self-sacrifice upon which the security and happiness of family life depend is on the decline. Only persons, particularly persons in families, can choose to restore it. Pressured perhaps by environmental concerns or the promptings of social justice, we can, as a nation, decide to become a bit more sparing and sharing. We can also choose to react to the increased pressures on family stability by caring more for others, particularly those with whom we share family life, and less for self. This will strengthen the family unit, and that, of course, means a strengthening of the larger society.

Affluence has had an atomizing and privatizing impact on contemporary American family life. Material progress has produced so many "private and personal" things—cars, rooms, cell phones, radios, TVs, stereos, computers, iPads and all the other hardware and software that make us less dependent on one another, but isolate us from close, physical, tangible contact at home, while enabling our isolated selves to reach out and electronically "touch" someone anywhere is the world.

With the brush of affluence, we seem to have painted ourselves, as family members and members of the larger society, into a very private but deeply lonely corner. How do we get out of that corner? The only way out is by coming together. Today's second reading (Col 3:12–13) points to an exit route from the self-enclosure that sometimes sets family members apart from one another:

"Put on, as God's chosen ones, holy and beloved, heartfelt compassion, kindness, humility, gentleness, and patience, bearing with one another and forgiving one another, if one has a grievance against another; as the Lord has forgiven you, so must you also do."

Forgiveness is the key. It has to be spoken, and when it is spoken in this Christmas season, it translates wisdom from the Book of Sirach (18:16) into a principle of family reinforcement: Sometimes, "a word can be better than a gift." A word of forgiveness can heal family wounds, tighten up family structures. Forgiveness means giving and restoring, reinstating and forgetting, when reinstatement and restoration are not deserved. The Letter to the Colossians calls us to forgive as the Lord has forgiven us. Who among us deserved the gift God gave us in Christ? Who can say he or she deserved the reconciliation with the Father that was achieved in the broken body of Christ? No one of us had any title at all to reinstatement in the life of grace, no claim to the forgiveness we have all received.

Aware of having been forgiven and yet still needing forgiveness in Jesus Christ, believers should extend to each other forgiveness now and the promise of future forgiveness. That, of course, is what it means to forgive as the Lord has forgiven you. Yet how unlike the Lord are so many members of so many families in the matter of forgiveness. How many of us say we forgive and stoutly refuse to forget, or let others forget? Who ever heard of forgiving a debt by requiring payment in full? And yet you can't help noticing, when families get together, how some members exact painfully full payment by inflicting sharp words or long silences, deep hurts and stinging sarcasm, on other members of the family. Sometimes this is preamble to the conferral, with great reluctance and no small measure of righteousness, of my forgiveness.

"As the Lord has forgiven, so must you also do."

The Feast of the Holy Family is as good a day as any, and better than most, to consider that God might be inviting you to walk on the path of forgiveness toward other members of your family from whom you may have separated yourself, if not spatially perhaps emotionally, psychologically, or spiritually. This could be healing time. With the healing comes a stronger family unit, and with that a stronger and better society.

I know this sounds idealistic and I realize that division and differences are part of any family life. Henri de Lubac's words (from his book, *Further Paradoxes*) have always made a lot of sense to me: "To differ, even deeply, from one another is not to be enemies; it is simply to be. To recognize and accept one's own difference is not pride. To recognize and accept the difference of others is not weakness. If union has to be, if union offers any meaning at all, it must be union between different people. And it is above all in the recognition and acceptance of difference that difference is overcome and union achieved." That, as I indicated, makes a lot of sense to me.

Another comment along these lines that makes a good deal of sense is the late Sam Rayburn's observation that "when two people always agree about everything, it just goes to prove that one of them is doing all the thinking!"

All happy families are alike in this regard; all happy families have differences that are not necessarily divisive and certainly not destructive. I'd find it reassuring, however, if more families would adopt those words I've already quoted from the Letter to the Colossians as kind of a family creed, or charter, or collective agenda. But what I quoted earlier is not the complete text of today's second reading. Listen now to the rest:

> And over all these put on love, that is, the bond of perfection. And let the peace of Christ control your hearts, the peace into which you were also called in one body. And be thankful. Let the word of Christ dwell in you richly, as in all wisdom you teach and admonish one another, singing psalms, hymns, and spiritual songs with gratitude in your hearts to God. And whatever you do, in word or in deed, do everything in the name of the Lord Jesus, giving thanks to God the Father through him (Col 3:14–17).

10

January 1, Octave of Christmas, Solemnity of Mary, Mother of God

"And Mary Kept All These Things, Reflecting on Them in Her Heart" (Luke 2:19)

Numbers 6:22–27; Psalm 67; Galatians 4:4–7; Luke 2:16–21

"And Mary kept all these things, reflecting on them in her heart." Think about "all these things" for a moment; try to put yourself in a reflective mode on this Feast of Mary the Mother of God, on this first day of our new year. Reflect awhile this morning.

I offer two points to assist you, two reflections written by others. One by St. Augustine; the other by the late Barbara Boggs Sigmund.

No one I've read communicates both the profundity and the simplicity of "these things," the things that Mary reflected upon as Luke suggests, than St. Augustine. In a beautiful expression of poetic wonder, Augustine wrote:

> When the Maker of time, the Word of the Father, was made flesh, He gave us His birthday in time; and He, without whose divine bidding no day runs its course, in His Incarnation reserved one day for Himself. He Himself with the Father precedes all spans of time; but on this day, issuing from His mother, He stepped into the tide of the years.
>
> ...And now, with what words shall we praise the love of God? What thanks shall we give? He so loved us that for our sakes He, through whom time was made, was made in time; and He, older by eternity that the world itself, was younger in age than many of His servants in the world; He who made man, was made man; He was given existence by a mother whom He brought into existence; He was carried in hands that He formed; He was nursed at breasts that

He filled; He cried like a babe in the manger in speechless infancy—
this Word without which human eloquence is speechless. (Christmas
homily, 5th century)

"And Mary kept all these things, reflecting on them in her heart."
And you, dear friends, can reflect today with Mary, the Mother of
God, and treasure these things in your own hearts.

Let me suggest that you also treasure Mary herself for what she is, God's
Mother and your mother. To assist you toward that end, let me quote for
you the words of a contemporary, the late Barbara Boggs Sigmund—
wife, mother, writer, poet, daughter of Hale and Lindy Boggs, sister of
the well-known television and public radio commentator Cokie Roberts,
and innovative mayor of Princeton, New Jersey, until she died of cancer
in 1990. Barbara Sigmund wrote a 1987 essay in *America* magazine entitled, "If I Had Five Minutes with the Pope," calling upon the pope to
"bring back Mary" to Catholic devotional life. She said:

> Modern women in particular need her to validate female strength-in-
> gentleness in the world of power. We are entering that world inexorably
> but uncertainly; jealous of both our femininity and our detachment.
> We resist taking on the "pinstripes of the oppressor," but all of our
> archetypes of power are male ones: the warrior, the team, the old bulls
> and the young. We need a model of our own on the grand scale.
>
> So bring back Mary…to celebrate the need for the tough
> tenderness of femaleness in the life of the world, to acknowledge that
> charm and kindness can still entice God to dwell among us.

How right she was. And there you have something all of us—male
and female, old and young, but especially those who are both young
and female—can reflect upon today, the naming day of Jesus and the
feast day honoring Mary's motherhood. Let us honor her by being ever
more devoted sons and daughters during this New Year.

11

Second Sunday after Christmas

In the Beginning

Sirach 24:1–4, 8–12; Psalm 147; Ephesians 1:3–6, 15–18; John 1:1–18

Let me suggest that you think about Christmas as a new beginning. It was a new beginning over two thousand years ago for the whole human race, to be sure, but think about it now as a new beginning for you, each one of you, in this Christmas season. It is Christmas. Think of it as something new, for you, this year.

The Fourth Gospel, the Gospel of St. John opens with these words: "In the beginning." "In the beginning was the Word." "*In principio erat verbum*" is the Latin version of that message that the elders among you will remember hearing in what was called the "Last Gospel" that used to be read at the end of every Mass before the liturgical changes that came after the Second Vatican Council.

> In the beginning was the Word,
>
> and the Word was with God,
>
> and the Word was God.
>
> He was in the beginning with God.
>
> All things came to be through him,
>
> and without him nothing came to be.
>
> What came to be through him was life,
>
> and this life was the light of the human race;
>
> the light shines in the darkness,
>
> and the darkness has not overcome it.

Reflect on what you just heard. The "Word," the *Verbum*, refers to Jesus Christ, the Second Person of our Triune God—Father, Son, and Holy Spirit. The divine Word, spoken, as it were, by the Father, is the Christ of Christmas. He was there at the beginning—before time, from all eternity—but not as Christ, rather as the Word, the creating Word of God.

It was not until the first Christmas night, the silent night, the holy night, that the divine Word, who had taken human flesh by the Holy Spirit in the womb of the Virgin Mary nine months previously, was born as Christ our Lord. Listen to the continuation of the prologue of St. John's Gospel:

He was in the world,

and the world came to be through him,

but the world did not know him.

He came to what was his own [i.e., to us, to you and me, to the human race],

but his own people did not accept him.

"But to those who did accept him he gave power to become children of God, to those who believe in his name, who were born not by natural generation nor by human choice nor by man's decision but of God." In other words, John is saying, to those who, like you and me, have been born again by faith, power is given to become children of God. You and I are thus empowered; we are adopted sons and daughters of the Triune God. And we celebrate at Christmastime the birth of the One who made this happen, who brought this about, who created our world and recreated us. So, St. John goes on to say in the concluding words of the prologue to his Gospel:

And the Word became flesh

and made his dwelling among us [the literal meaning of the Greek verb used by John is, "he pitched his tent among us"],

and we saw his glory,

the glory as of the Father's only Son,

full of grace and truth.

Those are truly remarkable as well as beautiful words. They are yours to ponder at this hour. Make them your own as you reflect on the meaning of Christmas as a new beginning this year for you.

I'd like to suggest three locations in your life, or three areas where a new beginning can take place right now. The first is *forgiveness*; the second is *family*, and the third is *giving*.

Forgiveness. When I mention that word, what comes immediately to your mind? Are you holding back right now, refusing to forgive someone, or refusing to forgive yourself? Or, are you too proud to ask another for forgiveness?

Consider how forgiveness and apology are first cousins; they live at opposite ends of the same street. Take a look at both ends of the street for a moment at Christmastime.

You may find it very hard to say, "I apologize," even when you know you should. Well, Christmas is the time to say that word. Whenever that word is spoken, it calls for a response in the vocabulary of forgiveness. Someone once said that "the singular achievement of [an apology]… resides in is capacity to effectively eradicate the consequences of the offense by evoking the unpredictable faculty of forgiveness." There's a very nice thought. Wonderful, isn't it, how certain words at certain times can make a problem disappear?

Are you refusing to forgive, when someone else says to you I'm sorry, I apologize? Or has your own expression of sorrow, your apology, fallen on deaf ears, not drawn the hoped-for response of forgiveness? As I said, forgiveness and apology are opposite ends on the same street. Christmas may be the time for you to take a walk up and down that street, to figure out where you are in your relationship with someone you may have hurt, or who may have hurt you, or figure out where you are in your relationship with yourself perhaps, and simply decide to say in faith and humility—in the true Christmas spirit—whatever it is that must be said, so that you can take your proper place in the Christmas celebration.

Forgive, as the Lord has forgiven you. Forgiveness is the foundation of the Christmas mystery. It is the reason why the Son of God took our flesh, was born, and "pitched his tent among us." Forgiveness.

The second area for thinking about a new beginning in your life at Christmastime is *family*. This is a family celebration, a family feast. Just being together as family is a source of strength and joy; or, at least, it should be. We acknowledge that Christmas carries an edge of sadness for those who lost a family member recently. Christmas can also see the rise of family tensions and pressures—that's why forgiveness is so important at this time of year.

But best of all, Christmas brings us back in touch with the Holy Family—Mary, Joseph and their infant Son—and just picturing them in the simple surroundings of the cave or stable in Bethlehem can serve to remind us moderns of the importance of simplicity to family life and love. There was nothing commercial about the first Christmas, nothing expensive, nothing stylish. There was just family love. And to the extent that we admit the expensive and the stylish, to the extent that the products of commerce find their way into our celebration of Christmas, we have to take great care that we do not permit ourselves to be possessed by our possessions, or obsessed with the material side of Christmas to the point of losing touch with the simplicity that makes it all so beautiful and full of meaning.

That brings me to my third point, the third location in your life where the new beginning of Christmas can find its way into your life—*generosity*.

You've been generous to others and others have been generous to you in the Christmas gift exchange. But think for a moment about the meaning of generosity. Surely, it is not a form of bribery. You don't purchase affection with your gifts. Surely, generosity is not a mask for lording it over others, dominating them with the power of your purse. Generosity puts the other person first. It is a way of opening your heart to another. Generosity is one way you have of affirming another.

Generosity is one way you have of imitating God. Generosity is an opportunity to be good just for the sake of being good.

You've heard it said that cleanliness is next to godliness, that to forgive is divine. Well consider how generosity can put you right up there with the giver of all gifts, on a plane with the good and generous creator of all we have. Your generosity can be your participation in divine creativity. Just let it happen. Just be generous. Let it be part of your new beginning in this Christmas season.

12

Epiphany

Epiphany: A Showing Forth

Isaiah 60:1–6; Psalm 72; Ephesians 3:2–3a, 5–6; Matthew 2:1–12

Epiphany marks the end of the Christmas season and the beginning of a renewed effort to "show forth," for all the world to notice, what it means to be a Christian.

"In times of extreme social and political distress, God is hidden; and it is the saint who makes God reappear," writes theologian Lawrence Cunningham in an essay on the saints. Some might want to argue that God is even less noticeable in times of prosperity. People enjoying security and affluence are all too easily distracted from God. They are less likely to acknowledge their need for God. They become like the affluent farm family in Jane Smiley's novel *A Thousand Acres*. "We went to church to pay our respects, not to give thanks," remarks the narrator-daughter of a family that successfully farmed unpromising land with the benefit of hard work, innovation, and application of expensive technology. With all that who needs God?

In either case—times of extreme social and political distress, or times of security and affluence that distract people from a consciousness of their dependence upon God—it is the saint who makes God reappear. Epiphany, therefore, occasions a reflection on the call to sanctity, to union with God, on the part of believers who are called to translate Christmas "fantasy" (the word is etymologically linked to "epiphany") into the other fifty-one weeks of the year.

The original Epiphany event introduced gift giving to the Nativity story; not necessarily to the celebration of Christmas as we know it (I'm not sure exactly when the custom of gift-exchange began), but to the New Testament narrative of the birth of Christ. With the Magi come the suggestion that we are called to a balance in our lives between matter and spirit. The material side is surely represented in their gifts, particularly the gold. The spiritual is also there. It is exhibited first in their readiness to respond to divine direction, to follow the star. It is also contained in the symbolism of the gift of incense (prayer, homage, respect) and myrrh (a gum resin with a bitter taste, prefiguring the bitter death the child would face as a man). Perhaps through a better balance of matter and spirit in contemporary Christian living, sanctity can become more evident in the world, thus enabling God to be seen a bit more clearly, to "reappear," in a manner of speaking, in our midst.

Isaiah's voice is heard again in the Epiphany liturgy: "...your light has come, the glory of the Lord shines upon you. Though darkness covers the earth, and thick clouds, the peoples. Upon you the LORD will dawn, and over you his glory will be seen." (Is 60:1–2). The words are repeated annually in the Epiphany liturgy because the Church wants you to hear them, and believe them, and apply them to yourself. "Upon you the LORD will dawn, and over you his glory will be seen." Who can say whether or not the emphasis was there "in the original," as the editorial notation would put it? It probably was. It certainly should be to the eye and ear of faith today.

You may feel at this moment, now that the decorations are down or coming down and perhaps, your spirits with them, that you are "walking in darkness." Or it may just be your stage in life or some troubling circumstance that has you down. You've got to believe that your Lord has broken through the darkness, dispersed the clouds and is shining now on you. You now have the job of letting him shine through you to others. That is saint's work, and that is what you, as a Christian, are called to do.

Let me tell you the story of a father who took his eight-year-old son into an empty church one bright sunny afternoon and walked him up and down the side aisles to "introduce" him to the saints who were depicted in the stained glass windows. The sun streamed through the colored glass and the father told the boy about St. Bernadette, St. Peter, St. Paul, St. Teresa, and all the others whose representations were there in the windows. Later that day the boy told a friend that he had been in church looking at the saints. "What's a saint?" asked his young friend. "A saint is someone the light shines through," replied the youngster.

Epiphany is a composite of two Greek words: *epi* and *phano*, meaning "to shine forth," to let your light "bump up against" the world.

Occasionally you hear the questions, "Did the Magi really exist?" "Was there really a star?" A sensible reply is that no one knows for sure with historical precision, and, for that matter, the literal truth of the story is unimportant. There were in fact Babylonian or Chaldean "wise men" in those days; there were also Persian "wise men" at the time of the birth of Christ. They were respected as astronomers and as what the Gospel story calls "astrologers." But the real question is: Why did the Holy Spirit want these elements included in the Gospel story? What is the religious or theological purpose of the story of the three Wise Men?

First, the story is there to stress the universality of Christ. He came not just to the Jews, but to the Gentiles (the *gentes*)—the other nations—as well. The Gospel story has him "showing himself forth" to the nations. It is an epiphany. St. Matthew's Gospel is also stressing the fact that Jesus is the messiah-king. The story thus serves the theological purpose of the author and that, of course, is fine. But what about us? What about the question the writings of Isaiah and Matthew raises for us today? "Your light has come…Upon you the Lord shines." What are the implications for us today?

Christ, the light of your life, is "out there," of course, in the world, your world. But he is also within you. You have always to be setting out, as the Magi did, to find him. Yours is both an outward and an inward journey—inwardly deepening your spirituality, outwardly spreading the good news. You've got a star to follow. That star is your vocation; it is visible in the circumstances of your life, the circumstances that help you define yourself—as husband or wife, father or mother, son or daughter, grandfather or grandmother, lawyer, broker, entrepreneur, driver, manager, civil servant, teacher, volunteer, student, businessperson, nurse, physician, programmer, designer, vowed religious, retiree [let those I've missed just fill in the blank!]—your circumstances are the context within which you find your calling. That's your star, your calling, your vocation. It is a moving star because the God who calls never stops calling and might, indeed, be calling you to something new! You have to follow that call, that star, to find Christ your Light, as the Magi did. And you find him only to pass him on, by word and example, to others.

As Christmas has now turned into Epiphany, and as Epiphany reopens the door to "ordinary time" and ordinary life, you can consider anew your opportunity to be a saint, to let that little light of yours shine and brighten your corner of a troubled world. "It is the saint," as Lawrence Cunningham indicated, "who makes God re-appear." And, by the way, the definition of a saint, as a friend of mine likes to remind me, "is a sinner who keeps on trying!"

Epiphany, everyone!

13

Baptism of the Lord

"You Are My Beloved Son; With You I Am Well Pleased"

Isaiah 42:1–4, 6–7; Psalm 29; Acts 10:34–38; Matthew 3:13–17.
[In Year C, these readings may be used: Isaiah 40:1–5, 9–11; Psalm
104; Titus 2:11–14; 3:4–7; Luke 3:15–16, 21–22]

On this Feast of the Baptism of the Lord, it is natural to ask: Why did Jesus have to be baptized? He was free of original sin; why did he present himself for baptism?

Well, first you have to remember that ritual washings were common when Jesus walked the earth and before he established his Church. They were rites of purification submitted to freely by mature persons who knew they weren't perfect and needed purification before God. These baptismal rites also represented something of an induction ceremony, a formal entrance into the community of those who believed in and honored God as their Father. The rite was called *baptism* because that word, the Greek verb *bapto*, means plunge or immerse. That's how this rite of immersing someone in river waters got the name of baptism.

John the Baptizer was so named because ritual purification was part of his prophetic ministry. He was a messenger, a prophet, an agent of God. He summoned people back to God. He called people to be obedient to God's commands. He helped people experience a rebirth through the waters of purification.

But Jesus didn't need to be purified, so why did he present himself for baptism? For several reasons: (1) as a young adult he wanted to be inducted into the faith community of his elders; (2) as the messiah missioned by God, he wanted to have this "inauguration" ceremony launch his public life; and (3) as the promised "one who is to come," he wanted to establish a formal connection between himself and his precursor, his advance man, Elizabeth's son John, who is known to all as John the Baptist.

Preachers and writers in the early Church would make much of the fact that Jesus, who needed no purification or sanctification, sanctified or blessed the water instead of the water of his baptism sanctifying him. For all who follow Christ, Christian baptism, with water that is sanctified by Jesus, is an initiation into the life and mystery of Christ, into the faith community that is the Church of Christ. The person like you and me who is baptized is symbolically and sacramentally plunged into the death of Jesus, so that we can rise with Jesus, we can come up out of the waters of baptism to walk in newness of life.

And notice that Mark's Gospel (Year B) says, "On coming up out of the water he [Jesus] saw the heavens being torn open and the Spirit, like a dove, descending upon him. And a voice came from the heavens, 'You are my beloved Son; with you I am well pleased.' " That is exactly what happened to each of you on the day of your baptism. The Holy Spirit descended upon you and God said of you: This is my beloved son, or my beloved daughter, with whom and in whom I am so well pleased. In another location in Scripture where these words are recorded, the voice of God the Father, speaking of Jesus, says "on him my favor rests." God's favor is God's grace. God's "favorites" are those who share God's life and love—those words describe God's grace—and that statement "on whom my favor rests" applies to every one of you.

"Oh, Lord I am not worthy," you might be saying to yourself right now. Of course, you're not worthy. You cannot earn God's love. It is a gift. You've received that gift. You are gifted, you are graced, and you should let the awareness of your divine giftedness sink into the depths of your soul today. Delight in it. Give thanks for it. Are you perfect? No. Are you lovable and loved by God? Indeed you are. Come up out of the waters; let the Lord God bring you up out of your sinfulness. Rise, by God's grace, above your sense of unworthiness and enjoy the assurance God gives you that you are indeed his beloved son or daughter. Believe that God is indeed pleased with you.

Sure, you've got a lot of room for improvement; you can get better. But remember, you don't have to be ill to get better. You're not ill; you are graced and healed and you do yourself no favor at all if you refuse to believe that God's favor rests on you!

So let that be the takeaway from this Gospel story today. God's favor rests on you. God is pleased with you.

You probably know that Pope John Paul II introduced a new set of five mysteries to be reflected upon when you pray the rosary. He calls them the luminous mysteries, or "mysteries of light" and they provide you with a fourth set to be added to the so-called joyful, sorrowful, and glorious mysteries of the rosary. John Paul II wanted Catholics to consider the "mysteries of light" when they recite the rosary on Saturdays.

Let me make two observations about this welcome innovation. First, you may never have noticed that the mysteries of the rosary, as you learned them years ago, were completely silent regarding the public life of Jesus. The fifth joyful mystery is the Finding of the Child Jesus in the Temple, and the first sorrowful mystery is the Agony in the Garden. The years of private and public life up till then are not brought to mind while praying the rosary, at least not until John Paul II introduced the mysteries of light.

The mysteries of light begin with the event of today's Gospel, the Baptism of the Lord. And the fourth mystery of light is the Transfiguration where again the heavens open and the voice of God is heard to say, "This is my beloved Son, with whom I am well pleased; listen to him" (Matthew 17:5). My hope is that Catholics throughout the world will reflect on these mysteries of light and that their prayerful reflection will help them assimilate the conviction that they are good, that God loves them, that God's grace makes them loved and lovable and that God is indeed pleased with them. Let that light go on in your inner house, in your soul, in your awareness.

The other three of the five mysteries of light are, by the way, (1) the proclamation by Jesus that the Kingdom of God is at hand, made after his baptism at the Jordan; (2) Cana; and (3) the Institution of the Eucharist. Each has a scriptural address. Each has an image you can file away in your mind. But most important of all, put yourself with Jesus today there at the Jordan, and because you are a Christian, let God's words spoken of him, apply as well to you: "You are my beloved Son [or daughter], with whom I am well pleased."

III
Lent

. . . .

14

First Sunday of Lent

The Temptations of Jesus

Deuteronomy 26:4–10; Psalm 91; Romans 10:8–13; Luke 4:1–13

"Filled with the Holy Spirit, Jesus returned from the Jordan and was led by the Spirit into the desert for forty days, to be tempted by the devil" (Luke 4:1). Let's take a moment to unpack that first sentence in today's Gospel reading from Luke. The story is an important one. It deals with temptation. Jesus suffered temptations; so do you. In observing Jesus you can make appropriate comparisons between him and yourself; you can also learn from his example some good preemptive and defensive strategies.

Notice that Jesus was "filled with the Holy Spirit," but not immune to temptation. So don't be surprised when temptation comes your way. And certainly don't conclude that God is absent when you are confronted with evil, evil that comes to you under the appearance of good. Don't think that you are evil because you may have evil tendencies. Don't think that the Holy Spirit is not with you when you are confronted by Satan, the enemy of your human nature. Satan does indeed exist; you and all who share your wonderful but fallen human nature have an enemy to deal with, a personal enemy, a diabolical force, an adversary, an oppositional principle of evil. But you needn't be afraid. Jesus was there before you. This enemy of your human nature can confront you even when you, like Jesus, are "filled with the Holy Spirit."

Luke tells you that Jesus was "led by the Spirit" into a desert place where he would be "tempted by the devil." Temptation was a reality in the life of Jesus; it will also be a reality in your life. His temptations are meant to be a comfort to you, a source of strength for you, a promise of the victory that will be yours. In a manner of speaking, his temptation overcomes your temptation, just as his death overcomes your death.

He fasted for forty days there in the desert. Why? Because he was drawn there by the Holy Spirit, prompted by the Spirit to prepare through this form of ascetical practice for his mission, to condition himself for the work that God had in mind for him. He was understandably weak and hungry at the end of forty days. He was vulnerable. And the devil hit him at his point of physical vulnerability. Satan hits Jesus at the level of basic need. This first temptation focuses on food. "If you are the Son of God, command this stone to become bread." Somehow or other Satan seems to be in charge here, but not in ultimate control. He has power and he is using it. But Jesus stands firm. Satan's stones-and-bread argument is "of the type which will always appeal to those who think of natural blessings as unequivocal signs of God's favor" (Vann and Meagher, The *Temptation of Christ*, Sheed & Ward, 1957, p. 64). We too easily forget that the good must sometimes suffer, but this in no way means that God has abandoned them. Satan seems to be trying to make Jesus feel sorry for himself. He needs bread. God is not providing. God does not care, doesn't appreciate, doesn't thank. As you and I might find ourselves saying, God is asking too much of me.

The first of these three temptations relates to the humanity of Christ. Jesus dismisses this temptation with the now famous words, "It is written, *'One does not live on bread alone.'*"

The second temptation targets the messianic work of Jesus, his mission. As Luke describes the situation, Satan took Jesus up "and showed him all the kingdoms of the world in a single instant. The devil said to him, 'I shall give to you all this power and glory; for it has been handed over to me, and I may give it to whomever I wish. All this will be yours, if you worship me.'" Think about that. Perhaps Graham Greene's book-title phrase comes to mind, *The Power and the Glory*. Perhaps you are prompted to ask that if, indeed, Satan had power to hand all this over to "whomever" he wished, who, in fact, did he give it to, figuratively speaking, who might be in possession now of this kind of worldly power? You might shiver a bit if your question yields a plausible answer, an answer that points to present possession and abuse of worldly power and glory. In any case, you can reply with Jesus: "It is written: *You shall worship the Lord, your God, and him alone shall you serve.*"

Now there is the beginning of an effective preemptive and preventative strategy for you.

So there was a temptation first to food, and now to power. Most modern Scripture scholars will tell you that Satan's purpose was to seduce Jesus from fulfilling the messianic ministry he was on the point of beginning, and from fulfilling it in the manner willed by the Father. Satan was suggesting that Jesus conform himself to the popular concept of the messiah. Those kind of temptations have or will surely come your way—to conform yourself to worldly ways, to this world's values.

Next Satan tempts Jesus in another way: he led him "to Jerusalem, made him stand on the parapet of the temple, and said to him: 'If you are the Son of God, throw yourself down from here, for it is written: *He will command his angels concerning you, to guard you,* and: *With their hands they will support you, lest you dash your foot against a stone.'"* This temptation relates to the use of divine power in the face of human insecurity. Why be afraid of falling when you know those angels will be there as a safety net? It is also a crass appeal to human vanity. Surely everyone will notice you if you pull off an extraordinary stunt like this. What better way to launch your public mission? But Jesus says to Satan in reply: "[It is also written that] *You shall not put the Lord, your God, to the test."*

With that, Satan left him. Christ responded to all three temptations out of his singleness of purpose, his compass was set. He stayed his course. All of this amounted to a temptation against vocation. The cunning serpent that was there at work in the Garden of Eden is at it again in this Gospel story. He'll be at it again in your own life. He tries to get you to suspect God's plan and substitute the wisdom of the world. "We were fooled by the wisdom of the serpent," St. Augustine once remarked, "but we were saved by the foolishness of God."

In each of these three scenes, Christ looked foolish to the earth-based worldly eye. You might think yourself foolish at times in fending off temptation. But divine foolishness has demonstrated its power to save the world. That power is available to you in your own moments of temptation.

Satan hit Jesus at his human points of vulnerability. You'll be hit there too from time to time. He'll work on your weak side, your tendency toward self-distrust, discouragement, self-denigration; he'll try to find an opening through your sense of unworthiness, even self-hatred. If, as your mother told you years ago, "Idle hands are the devil's workshop," this Gospel story is telling you today that human discouragement is the devil's playground.

Keep your eye on Christ. Don't fall into a pattern of feeling sorry for yourself at the end of whatever forty days of frustration and hardship that might come your way. Accept the affirmation of God's love and retain your balance with the wisdom that a sense of your own fallibility and weakness can bring. We are all wounded healers as we struggle to help one another. We all need strength in the face of temptation. We find that strength in the example of Christ.

15

Second Sunday of Lent

"Enemies of the Cross of Christ"

Genesis 15:5–12, 17–18; Psalm 27; Philippians 3:17—4:1;
Luke 9:28b–36

You may have been struck by an expression St. Paul uses in today's selection from his letter to the Philippians. I know I was. I've been intrigued by this expression for many years. Paul writes that "many... conduct themselves as enemies of the cross of Christ. Their end is destruction. Their God is their stomach; their glory is in their 'shame.' Their minds are occupied with earthly things."

"Enemies of the cross of Christ." He's not speaking of outright enemies—adversaries, hostile forces arrayed against the person and mission of Jesus. No, Paul has in mind a more subtle enemy influence, a stubborn clinging to the old Jewish food laws (hence the reference to the "stomach") and their boasting of circumcision which, in Paul's view, is to "glory" in something that otherwise modesty would cover. All of these Old Law things are now superseded, displaced, by Christ. These men and women who are "enemies" of his new way, his way of the cross, will not let go.

By extension to people like you and me, this message suggests that unwittingly, unconsciously, we can conduct ourselves as if we were, in fact, enemies of the cross of Christ. And for some of the same reasons. We can become so locked into traditional ways of thinking and acting that we close ourselves to the new. Or, to use another Pauline phrase, we can effectively "stifle the Spirit."

"Their God," says Paul, "is their stomach." Sometimes our stomachs control our better selves and we should pay attention to that during Lent. "Their minds are occupied with earthly things," wrote Paul. We know that problem—been there, done that, as they say. We forget that our "citizenship is in heaven" and we subscribe to earthbound values and behave arrogantly and immodestly as if we want only the earth to notice us. All too often there is little space in our lives for the values of the cross and thus we become, unwittingly, unconsciously, "enemies of the cross of Christ."

"The consolation is this," wrote Dorothy Day in her book *Loaves and Fishes*, "and this our faith too: by our suffering and our failures, by our acceptance of the Cross, we unleash forces that help to overcome the evil in the world." True. But how easily we forget. How easily we permit ourselves to misread both suffering and failure in our lives and thus become "enemies of the cross of Christ."

It happens in other ways too.

"They crucified him," the Scriptures say. You will recall and relive those words liturgically again this year during Holy Week. "They crucified him." But who are they? Don't be too hasty in answering that question. Sure, the crowd called out for his crucifixion. Pilate, the chief priest, the scribes—they all were there. But I'm part of the answer to the "who were they?" question. I am they—to the extent that I let myself become an enemy of the cross of Christ, to the extent that my way is not the way of the cross, to the extent that my values are not the values of Christ who gave himself up for me.

In its Holy Week liturgy, the Church puts these words from Psalm 69 on the lips of Jesus: "My heart dreaded reproach and misery, and I looked for someone to sympathize with me, but there was none. I sought for someone to comfort me, and I found none." Where was I while he was suffering? In the mysterious economy of grace I can choose *now* to offer sympathy and comfort *then*. Not only by being with and for Christ in my poor, suffering brothers and sisters in the human community today, if I choose to be there with them and see Christ in them, but I can sympathize and comfort Christ by simply choosing not to be an "enemy" of his cross in the way I live my life now.

Note again that in this segment we've been considering from the Letter to the Philippians, Paul is talking about those whose "minds are occupied with earthly things." For us who are so set upon the things of this world, St. John Chrysostom had some very stern remarks in a sermon he gave many centuries ago on a text (Jn 18:1–36) that described the sufferings and crucifixion of Jesus:

And you, O man, on hearing these things and seeing your Lord driven in fetters from place to place, have no esteem for the present life. Is it not a strange thing indeed, if Christ has undergone such strange sufferings for your sake, whereas you frequently cannot even bear up under harsh words? But he, on the other hand was spat upon, whereas you adorn yourself with fine apparel and rings, and, if you do not meet with words of approval from all men, you consider life not worth living. (Homily 83)

In so many small and subtle ways, any one of us can show himself or herself to be an enemy of the cross of Christ. The realization of this possibility should make us pause, here while it is still early in the Lenten season, for some spiritual stocktaking.

When you are jealous, petty, spiteful, envious, judgmental; when you seek revenge; when you delight in the misfortunes of others, you are showing yourself to be an enemy of the cross of Christ. Those actions stem from values that are too much "occupied with earthly things." If there have been in your personal experience any recent angers, outbursts, discouragements, or hurt feelings, examine the extent to which these may have sprung from a mind or heart that is too much set on earthly things, grounded in values that are not the values of Christ.

When you snap back at someone; when you cover up your own inadequacies by criticizing others; when you damage another's reputation; when you respond to criticism with anger, to advice with insult, to the truth about yourself with scorn for the bearer of that truth, you are showing yourself to be an enemy of the cross of Christ. These are the things you should be fasting from during Lent; fast from sin!

Don't let yourself get discouraged, however, as dull, cloudy, cold days of March close in on you. Don't get discouraged when Lenten observance becomes a bit heavy despite your best efforts. This is why the Church offers for your consideration the great Gospel story of the Transfiguration now that you are into the observance of Lent. There is light at the end of the tunnel. Not only have you picked a winner in Christ, but that winner has picked you. So put yourself in place there with Peter, John, and James, and look with gratitude to Jesus. "This is my chosen Son," said that voice from the heavens, "listen to him." Hear that same voice, the voice of God, speak directly of and to you this morning saying, "This is my beloved son, my beloved daughter, whom I love and in whom I am so well pleased!" Carry on with courage in your Lenten preparation for the celebration of the Easter victory!

16

Third Sunday of Lent

The Burning Bush

Exodus 3:1–8a, 13–15; Psalm 103; 1 Corinthians 10:1–6, 10–12;
Luke 13:1–9

This morning's first reading from the Book of Exodus has an angel of the Lord appearing to Moses "in fire flaming out of a bush." The bush, although on fire, was not consumed.

So Moses decided to walk over to the bush and take a closer look. The Scripture passage tells you, "When the Lord saw him coming over to look at it more closely, God called out to him from the bush, 'Moses, Moses.' " Now it is God's voice, not the angel's that calls from inside the burning bush. God calls Moses by name. And Moses says, "Here I am."

"God said, 'Come no nearer! Remove the sandals from your feet, for the place where you stand is holy ground. I am the God of your fathers.' " He continued, "the God of Abraham, the God of Isaac, the God of Jacob." Moses "hid his face," the Scripture tells us, "for he was afraid to look at God."

Then, as you remember, God told Moses that he was there to rescue his chosen people from the hands of the Egyptians and to lead them out of bondage into a land "flowing with milk and honey." And Moses, you will recall, asked God how, when he, Moses, went to the Israelites, he should identify God, what name should he give them. "God replied: 'I am who am....This is what you shall tell the Israelites: 'I AM sent me to you.' " "This is my name forever; thus am I to be remembered through all generations."

Well here we are—our generation, just one in the flow of so many generations—and this is how we should name and think of our God, as "I AM."

God is in our midst. Somehow or other we should be able to seek and find God in all things. God is in us, and around us, in front of us, behind us, beside us. There are "burning bushes" around us and we must take care that we not just walk by without noticing God, without "seeing" or "hearing" God present to us in our world.

The English poet Elizabeth Barrett Browning (1806–1861) pondered this biblical scene and wrote these lovely words:

Earth's crammed with heaven,

And every common bush afire with God;

But only he who sees, takes off his shoes—

The rest sit round it and pluck blackberries...

This is a beautiful spiritual insight that illumines the story of Moses and the burning bush and gives each one of us something to think about this morning.

The opening words of this biblical story from Exodus have been paraphrased this way: "Once there was a man [Moses] and a mountain [Horeb]. And the man walked upon the mountain and tended sheep there, and thought of common things. But one day, the man saw an uncommon sight. A bush burned nearby, and yet was not burned up. And the man did not pass by" ("Earth's Crammed with Heaven," Denise Cumbee Long, North Raleigh United Church, October 24, 1999).

"And the man did not pass by." Moses recognized that there was something extraordinary there. He saw the burning bush as a sign pointing him to the living presence of God.

To what extent are we walking by, passing and not noticing the presence of God in the burning bushes of our surroundings? "Earth's crammed with heaven / And every common bush afire with God." How many common bushes go unnoticed in our experience? As Elizabeth Barrett Browning noted, "Only he who sees takes off his shoes." Only those whose vision is spiritually acute can notice the divinity in simple things, ordinary things, common things. Only those who see with the soul's eye can hope to find God in all things, in all persons. We have to learn to look with wonder at our ordinary, but mysteriously wonderful, circumstances and surroundings. Bushes are burning all around us. We all too often don't even think about removing our shoes; we idly eat the blackberries!

If you are willing to concede that God is everywhere, then you should be open to having at least fleeting experiences of God's presence in your life, in your flesh-and-blood existence here on earth. Your burning bushes will almost always be ordinary events, ordinary people. Just remember that "earth's crammed with heaven / And every common bush afire with God." Pray that God will give you eyes to see and hearts to respond with reverence, awe, and wonder to God's presence in your life and in your midst.

And remember that the God to whom you pray is "I AM." God is existence; in all existence, therefore, you can find God. Your existence, your vitality reflects God's glory. God revealed himself to Moses as existence. Tell them that "I AM sent me to you," said God to Moses and he added: "This is my name forever; thus am I to be remembered through all generations."

Well, perhaps you have not remembered your God that way, as existence, as present in you and all around you. Perhaps the Church puts these readings before your mind today to awaken you, to bring you, so to speak, to your senses—your spiritual sense of sight, to sharpen your vision to the presence of God.

Take the Gospel warning in that context. Apply to yourself the warning Jesus gave not as a threat of eternal punishment, but as a lament that you are missing something. Jesus said, "I tell you, if you do not repent, you will all perish...." He repeats those words in the short selection you just heard from Luke's Gospel: "I tell you, if you do not repent, you will all perish." And then he tells you the parable of the fig tree—unproductive, yielding no fruit for three years. Apparently the tree was unattended, for the gardener asked the owner to give him another year—to cultivate the ground around the fig tree and to fertilize it. After that, if the tree fails to bear fruit, the gardener concedes that it will be all right to cut it down.

So might it be with us.

Give us time, Lord, to cultivate our sensitivity to your presence in ordinary things in the world around us, to notice that "every common bush is afire with God." And move us, Lord, to experience reverence in your presence, to be in awe of the creation in which we find you—in bushes, in city streets and in the faces of street people, in the sun and moon, in fields and streams, in gardens and gardeners. In sky and clouds, in both the bright and dark moments of life, you live, Lord, you who told us that your name is "I am who am," and who said, "This is my name forever; thus I am to be remembered through all generations."

Keep us alert to your presence, Lord; help us to remember.

17

Fourth Sunday of Lent

The Prodigal Son

Joshua 5:9a, 10–12; Psalm 34; 2 Corinthians 5:17–21;
Luke 15:1–3, 11–32

There are two abiding and important religious questions, both significant but one more important than the other, that we tend to confuse
in their order of importance. The first is "What is God like?" This is
a theological question of enormous importance, an exploration into
God, an important question to be investigated reverently in prayer and
systematically in study and reflection. The second important question
is "What must I do? How must I behave?" This is a question of moral
theology, of religious ethics, a question of moral right and wrong.

Most of us tend to put the second question first and to leave the
exploration into God for others who are more prayerful, more intel-
lectual, and, presumably, more faithful. We want to make sure, of
course, that we live within the moral boundaries, do the right thing,
do good and avoid evil, often more concerned with avoiding evil than
doing good. Avoiding evil, of course, is not unimportant, but if we
become preoccupied, or worse, *obsessed* with considerations of avoiding both evil and error, we might just be missing the progress God
wants us to make on the path of a growing awareness of how good
God is and how much God loves us for ourselves, not for what we do
(or fail to do).

Today's Gospel story of the Prodigal Son tells us a lot about what
God is like. Some would call it the story of the Prodigal Father because
it presents for our consideration a wonderfully generous, warm, forgiving, understanding father who runs out and literally trips over himself
in his hurry to gather up an errant son in a forgiving embrace. Jesus is
painting a portrait in this story, a portrait of his Father. Jesus is telling
us here what God is really like.

We tend to see ourselves in either or both of the two sons. The younger son—rebellious, irresponsible, soft of character, sensuous, and self-centered. The older son—judgmental, unforgiving, proud of his seniority, his record, his hardheaded (and hardhearted) loyalty. The father loves them both. Listen again to what he says to the older son toward the end of this story when the older son bitterly complains about the father's outpouring of generosity to the wayward younger son. "My son," the father says to the older brother, "you are here with me always; everything I have is yours." Let those words work themselves into your consciousness, those of you, and that would be just about all of you, who have not "squandered" your "inheritance on a life of dissipation." Your Father is saying to you today, "My son (my daughter), you are here with me always; everything I have is yours." Take him at his word. Listen and believe.

You can, of course, get a glimpse of yourself—real or exaggerated—in the younger son. Your wanderings, your unworthiness, your excesses may be in the forefront of your mind. God your Father is looking at you now and saying, in effect, "Quickly bring the finest robe and put it on him; put a ring on his finger and sandals on his feet. Take the fattened calf and slaughter it. The let us celebrate with a feast, because this son of mine was dead, and has come to life again; he was lost, and has been found." A feast, a celebration; for you? Yes, for you.

Tucked away in the middle of today's second reading from Second Corinthians (5:17–21) lies a clue to the reason why we fail to accept ourselves as "loved sinners," as sons and daughters of a loving Father who is always ready to forgive and forget, who has in fact forgiven you and forgotten your confessed foolishness, your sins, your faithlessness. The clue I'm referring to lies in these words: "[B]e reconciled to God. For our sake he [God] made him [Christ] to be sin who did not know sin, so that we might become the righteousness of God in him [Christ]." I like the way the *Jerusalem Bible* translates this verse into English: "[B]e reconciled to God. For our sake, God made the sinless one into sin, so that in him we might become the goodness of God" (2 Cor 5:21).

There you have it. By God's grace, you've been transformed into the goodness of God. Who me? Yes, you—you are the goodness of God.

If you have trouble accepting that fact, then you don't know what grace is. If you find yourself saying, "Well, that could be true of him, or she certainly fits that description, but not me, no never me; I'm not worthy, I'm just not good enough." If that is your reaction, then you've got some pondering to do, some meditating to do on these inspired words from Sacred Scripture.

Shortly after I was ordained to the priesthood back in 1961, a much older and wiser priest told me, "One of the most difficult jobs you're going to have as a priest is to convince people that God loves them." That sounded quite strange to me then; it is not at all strange now. I've had plenty of experience of the difficulty of persuading people that God loves them. What a pity. How much they lose—how much more peace of soul, happiness, spiritual contentment, balance, and sense of purpose would be theirs, if they would simply accept the fact that God loves them.

And how much more lovable they themselves would be if they accepted themselves as loved sinners.

Some Lenten programs of "penance" are really quite secular, worldly, self-improvement programs—dieting, for example. I heard of one just the other day: "Slim for Him!" Well today, let me suggest that you give this program of reflection a try. If it works, it will become for you a genuine self-improvement program. Take God at his word; reflect on his word: "My son, you are here with me always; everything I have is yours." And again, "God made the sinless one into sin so that, in him, we might become the goodness of God." Believe that and you'll come to accept yourself as a loved sinner. With that acceptance will come a deep experience of Easter joy.

I hope all this makes you feel good; I pray that it will not let you feel complacent. God made his covenant with a people, with all of us together, not with an individual sinful you or me. We are a loved "us," a people set apart. Your exploration into God must not stop with an awareness simply of who God is and how God relates to you. It must not rest complacently on a Jesus-and-I island of isolated personal piety. Remember, there are two fundamentally and important religious questions—two: (1) What is God like? and (2) How must I behave, what must I do, what are my moral obligations? Once you locate yourself as a "loved sinner" and enjoy the reassurance, even the security that this realization brings, you have to look outward, especially to others in the human community who stand in need of your help. You have to start thinking of charity and justice.

You can never go to God alone. Not in prayer, not in pious practices, not in your eventual trip home to heaven. You cannot go home to God alone. In your heart, in your preoccupations, in your helping hands, there must be others, your brothers and sisters in the human community, especially your brothers and sisters who are both in need and within reach of your helping hand. You have obligations to them in charity and in justice.

What is God like? Look at him in the story of the Prodigal Father.

What must I do, how must I behave? Let the Lord instruct you on that point in your prayer today. Just for fun—theological fun if you will—look for an answer to that action question in what your imagination might suggest occupied the thoughts and actions of this Prodigal Son who, once reconciled with his father, had the rest of his life to live out in gratitude. He surely felt "much obliged." Imagine what he then proceeded to do for others.

With his restored right relationship to his father, he could not yet fly. He needed another wing, namely, a right relationship with all of his companions in the human community—rich and poor, black and white, brown and yellow, young and old, troublesome and trouble-free.

"My son, [my daughter], you are with me always; everything I have is yours." You can't say thanks to God for this without saying thanks to your neighbor.

18

Fifth Sunday of Lent

The Woman Taken in Adultery

Isaiah 43:16–21; Psalm 126; Philippians 3:8–14; John 8:1–11

You sometimes hear references to the Bible as constituting "great literature." Today's Gospel story is an exquisite piece of literature, a great story, a moving narrative about a sinful woman encountering a sensitive, compassionate, and merciful Jesus, who is always ready to forgive; and who, in this instance, displays great tact as well as deep compassion toward the woman taken in adultery.

Notice that the story begins with the simple description of Jesus sitting down in the midst of a small gathering of people in the temple area where he "began to teach them." You are sitting in on a class, so to speak; you are observing and listening to a master teacher at work!

Recall that adultery was, in that time and culture, a misdeed that merited punishment by stoning, stoning even unto death. There may have been, even then, a certain uneasiness about participating in capital punishment because it is virtually impossible to say, when a crowd throws the stones, who it is that causes the death of the victim. At any rate, we are in a story context that is not unfamiliar to those who listen to Jesus. They knew what punishment by stoning was all about.

Enter the scribes and Pharisees, the "righteous ones," the law-and-order crowd. With them comes a humiliated woman who had been "caught in the act of adultery." There were witnesses to this crime. The righteous "holier-than-thou" scribes and Pharisees led the woman forward. They made her stand there in front of everyone. They set the stage—this open-air courtroom stage—and they try to make Jesus an unwilling judge. "What do you say?" they ask. As the Gospel story notes, "they said this to test him, so that they could have some charge to bring against him."

Jesus reacts in a strange way. He simply bent down and started tracing on the ground with his finger. Take a moment now to try to picture the scene. You see a crowd of onlookers, a humiliated woman, the flinty-eyed scribes and Pharisees, and an apparently distracted Jesus scribbling in the soil. What do you think he could have been writing? Some suggest that he was jotting down the crimes of the onlookers, including the lapses of the righteous ones who were doing all the accusing. Maybe. We can't say for sure. Perhaps he was just doodling, idling away the time. In any case, while the others persisted in their questioning, Jesus straightened up, looked around, and said: "Let the one among you who is without sin be the first to throw a stone at her."

What a clever move. Brilliant! Then, he bent down and wrote on the ground again. Gradually, "they went away one by one, beginning with the elders." The lesson was getting through. Don't be so quick to condemn, especially when you might not be so blameless as you pretend to be. Temper justice with mercy. Lighten up is what Jesus seems to be saying to this crowd as he continued to scribble on the ground.

Eventually, Jesus straightens up once again, now, the Gospel story says, he is "alone with the woman." Dare to put yourself in that place at this moment. Regardless of whether you are a man or a woman, slip into her sandals; stand on her ground face-to-face with Jesus. Have a face-to-face encounter with the Lord. What might he want to say to you today?

If you are in need of forgiveness, he will surely offer that. If you are sad, he can bring joy. If you are anxious, he can calm you, eliminate your fears; just let him be present to you. This is an exercise of faith, not fantasy, that I am recommending to you now. Just let yourself slip out of yourself in faith and into the reassuring arms of your Savior.

He may well want to ask you, as he asked the woman in this story: "Where are those who were accusing you? Or, better, where are the worries that were bothering you? If no one is here now to condemn you, why are you condemning yourself? Why are you so hard on yourself?"

Feel him give you an encouraging pat on the back. Hear him send you off with a reassuring word: "Sin no more and rest assured that your faith, which is my gift to you, will remain with you and sustain you in all your reversals. Remain in my friendship and I will never let you go."

19

Passion Sunday (Palm Sunday)

"He Emptied Himself"

Isaiah 50:4–7; Psalm 22; Philippians 2:6–11;
Luke 22:14—23:56

After the annual proclamation of the Passion of the Lord, a homilist must take care to be attentive to an often–neglected wisdom principle, namely, that to add is to subtract. Let me simply attempt to extend this proclamation, as any homily should, by underscoring phrases from the first two readings from Scripture that were proclaimed by way of introduction to the Passion narrative. These phrases can help connect you to the Passion narrative in a personal way.

Isaiah told you in the opening reading that the Lord has given him "a well-trained tongue, that I might know how to answer the weary a word that will waken them." Among those words were these that fit so well on the lips of the Jesus you just followed on his way of the cross, words that apply to you in your weariness, in your effort to follow faithfully your Lord on your own way of the cross: "The Lord GOD is my help, therefore I am not disgraced; therefore I have set my face like flint, knowing that I shall not be put to shame."

Set your face like flint.

Believe that you shall never be disgraced if you follow him.

Know that you shall never be put to shame.

And the second reading—the Christological hymn in Paul's great Letter to the Philippians—tells you what you observed again this year with your mind's eye as you followed your Savior on his way of the cross. He "did not regard equality with God something to be grasped"

69

("to be clung to as a miser clings to his booty," in Joseph Fitzmyer's translation). He didn't stand on rank or privilege; he didn't "lord it over" anyone.

"Rather," says St. Paul, "he emptied himself, taking the form of a slave, coming in human likeness; and found human in appearance, he humbled himself, becoming obedient to death, even death on a cross."

> He emptied himself.
>
> He humbled himself.
>
> And just because he did it for us all, is no reason not to say that he did it all for you, just for you.
>
> He did it all for you.
>
> He would have done it just for you, had no one else but you had need of salvation.

But the fact is, we all stood in need of salvation. All of us of all ages, all colors, all races, all nations, all times, all circumstances—all of us were saved by his cross.

Living now, as we do, under the banner of the cross, we must empty ourselves, humble ourselves, and open ourselves in gratitude to God who saved us in Christ. We show our gratitude by extending ourselves in grateful service to our brothers and sisters in the human community, our brothers and sisters for whom Christ suffered the indignities and death that the Passion according to Luke has helped us to recall.

IV
Triduum

. . . .

20

Holy Thursday: Mass of the Lord's Supper

We Are Expected to Wash One Another's Feet

Exodus 12:1–8, 11–14; Psalm 116; 1 Corinthians 11:23–26;
John 13:1–15

This Holy Thursday can, quite literally, speak for itself. A homily is not inappropriate, of course, but if the liturgy for the Feast of the Lord's Supper is done well, the homily—always an extension of the proclamation—is less important than what you witness and hear. You will see, for example, the "washing of the feet," recalling the action Jesus performed on the night before he died, the night when he ate the Passover supper with his closest friends, the night he instructed them in what we have come to call his "farewell discourse," the night of the institution of the Holy Eucharist, the night when we were invited to do all this in his memory.

Accordingly, I have three points:

First, our symbolic washing of the feet in this liturgy should serve to remind that we, in imitation of Christ, are called to wash each other's feet. We are called to service. Our Lord and Savior, "did not come to be served but to serve and to give his life as a ransom for many." We know that. We are the beneficiaries of that paid ransom. In our freedom, we have chosen to follow Christ. And this Holy Thursday liturgy reminds us that following Christ means serving others. It means putting ourselves second and others first. It means humility in the presence of others. It means service where there is need.

Scholars describe the setting for the Last Supper as something of a semicircular fanning out, a spread of the participants on the floor around a low table; not a table-and-chair arrangement with which we are so familiar and which religious art and the eye of the imagination usually applies to the Last Supper setting. The point to note is that the apostles were stretched out, head toward the low-slung table, resting on their elbows, their feet out on the edge of the semicircle. It was therefore relatively easy for Jesus to move from one to the other, around the edge of the circle, with bowl and towel, washing their feet—an action of humble service. In any case, our ritual renewal of that action tonight is more formal and more awkward, but a reminder nonetheless, that we are expected to wash one another's feet, a symbolic way of acknowledging that we are called to love one another. Jesus will make that lesson specific in his own words a little later on.

For now, savor the scene and try to assimilate the lesson. We belong to a hierarchical Church, we know, but we are not expected to "lord it over" one another. All of us—even those with titles and power, and some measure of prestige—are foot washers. Before God, no one of us is "above" any other; all of us are on the same level, on the ground, where the foot meets the earth and gets dirty on the way, and is thus in need of the washing that each of us is expected to provide.

My second point is taken from the second reading, the selection you heard from Paul's first letter to the Corinthians. Paul recounts what he "received from the Lord," namely, "that the Lord Jesus, on the night in which he was handed over, took bread, and, after he had given thanks, broke it and said, "This is my body that is for you. Do this in remembrance of me." What was the "this" that they were to do in remembrance of him? It was the breaking of the bread and, of course, passing it around. "In the same way also the cup, after supper, saying, 'This cup is the new covenant in my blood. Do this, as often as you drink it, in remembrance of me.'"

In effect, Jesus was saying to those closest and dearest to him that they should not only remember him in the breaking of the bread and pouring out of the cup, but that they themselves should become bread broken for the nourishment of one another, and cups poured out in sacrifice for one another. "When we eat this bread and drink this cup, we proclaim your death, Lord Jesus, until you come in glory." That familiar liturgical acclamation is rooted directly in the words St. Paul used at the end of the reading you just heard: "For as often as you eat this bread and drink this cup, you proclaim the death of the Lord until he comes."

Just outside Philadelphia, in a suburb called Bryn Mawr, there is a sign along the road that identifies the church building at that location as the "Proclamation Presbyterian Church." I think that is a great idea—identifying the local church for what it is, a proclamation. Paul is instructing you here tonight to be just that—a proclamation. He is suggesting that you can make that proclamation by being bread broken for one another, by being a cup poured out for others. These Eucharistic symbols are sacramental signs. They do not merely symbolize; they are the body and blood, soul and divinity of Jesus, the God-man. Your lives point to him. Your deeds proclaim that he is alive and well and working in our midst. Your lives are a continuation of his proclamation.

And my third point takes you just a bit beyond the selection you have from the Gospel of John. The segment I read a few moments ago took you through the washing of the disciples' feet and left you with this lesson: "Do you realize what I have done for you [the washing of their feet]? You call me 'teacher' and 'master,' and rightly so, for indeed I am. If I, therefore, the master and teacher, have washed your feet, you ought to wash one another's feet. I have given you a model to follow, so that as I have done for you, you should also do."

As John's Gospel account moves beyond the point at which the selection for this liturgy ends, Jesus said to his friends, "I will be with you only a little while longer," and he continued: "I give you a new commandment: love one another. As I have loved you, so you also should love one another. This is how all will know that you are my disciples, if you have love for one another."

There you have the New Commandment. The Old Commandment, part of the Old Law, the Torah, would have you love your neighbor as you love yourself. That is not enough, says Jesus now, you must not be content with an ethic of reciprocity—loving others as they love you; now you are under an ethic of renunciation, an obligation to love as Christ loved you, to the point of laying down your life for the other. This is revolutionary Christianity—self-sacrificing love patterned on the love Christ had for us. Once this catches on, ours will be a new and better world. This was the revolution Christ came to launch; this is a revolution waiting to happen. And it cannot happen without you.

21

Good Friday: The Passion of the Lord

Woman, Behold, Your Son

Isaiah 52:13—53:12; Psalm 31; Hebrews 4:14–16; 5:7–9;
John 18:1—19:42

"When Jesus saw his mother and the disciple there whom he loved, he said to his mother, 'Woman, behold, your son.' Then he said to the disciple, 'Behold, your mother.' And from that hour the disciple took her into his home."

Standing, as we are this afternoon, at the foot of the cross—a station, had we been alive on that fateful Friday afternoon, we probably would not have had the courage to take—standing there now in faith, we hear Jesus speak (through John) to us: "Behold, your mother." We hear him directing her attention to us, saying to her in effect, "Behold your sons and daughters; be mother to them, care for them."

Here, at the foot of the cross on the hill of Calvary, another scene will develop shortly. Another image will emerge. I invite you to take that image to yourself now with your mind's eye, welcome it into memory and imagination. It is the image of the famous Michelangelo masterpiece, the *Pietá*. In that exquisite sculpture you find, carved in marble, a moving representation of pity and sorrow. You see Mary burdened with the weight of her dead Son stretched across her lap. She is burdened with the weight of sorrow and yet at peace as she gazes at the lifeless body of him whose promise extended to her, as well as to you and me, that we were all to learn of him, of his gentleness, of his humility, and with those lessons learned, she (Mary), you and I, all of us, would not find life burdensome. Remember the promise? "Take my yoke upon you and learn from me, for I am meek [gentle] and humble of heart; and you will find rest for your selves. For my yoke is easy, and my burden light."

That was and is a promise of Christ to Mary, his first follower, and to all of us who would follow later, that we would—by knowing and learning from Christ—that we would achieve an abiding sense of peace despite the weight of life's burdens.

In the Christmas season, you saw the image of the Madonna and Child, the young mother and the baby at the beginning of that baby's life on earth. In the *Pietá*, you see the end, the end of an earthly journey of thirty-three years. In this artistic presentation, Mary's Son, the Son of God, is once again on her lap.

All who look on Michelangelo's *Pietá* can see how insupportably heavy is the body of her dead Son on Mary's lap. And looking at her sculpted features we can also see how much heavier was the burden in her heart. The genius of Michelangelo combined two life-size figures in one sculpture, carved from one block of marble. Both figures are bathed in tranquility. The Mother can see and weep; the Son's eyes are closed in death. The Mother can also hope, and the Son, as we now know, did indeed rise again.

Today, dear friends, we gather as a remembering people. We gather also as a people of hope. In the silent sadness of the *Pietá*, we see both hope and the promise of resurrection.

We now find ourselves perhaps yoked and burdened with the cares of life, but we know that by the power of Christ's Resurrection, the yoke will become easy, the burden will be lightened through our faith-based participation in the victory of the risen Jesus.

We believe the eternal truth communicated by Paul to the Romans, "If God is for us, who can be against us?...It is Christ [Jesus] who died, rather, was raised, who also is at the right hand of God, who indeed intercedes for us. What will separate us from the love of Christ?" (Rom 8:31ff.) We answer that question from the depths of our sad but faith-filled hearts with one word: Nothing. Let nothing, we pray, ever separate us from the love of Christ

It was the love of Christ on the cross that entrusted us to his Mother. The love of Christ commended her to us. Her love for us is at work in us today.

"When Jesus saw his mother and the disciple there whom he loved, he said to his mother, 'Woman, behold, your son.' Then he said to the disciple, 'Behold, your mother.' And from that hour the disciple took her into his home." Take her to your home. Let her take you to her Son.

An ancient hymn of the Church connects these stations and links them antiphonally with the words, "Have mercy, O Lord, have mercy on us!" Permit me to repeat that hymn now and I ask you to respond as indicated with the connecting antiphon:

O Lord Jesus Christ,

At prayer in the Garden of Olives,

Weeping with sadness and fear,
Comforted by an Angel.

antiphon—Have mercy, O Lord, have mercy on us!

O Lord Jesus Christ,

Betrayed by the kiss of Judas,

Abandoned by your apostles,
Delivered over to sinners.

antiphon—

O Lord Jesus Christ,

Buffeted, covered with spittle,

Bruised by the blows of soldiers,
Condemned to die on the cross.

antiphon—

O Lord Jesus Christ,

Scourged and crowned with thorns,

Clothed in a robe of purple,

Covered with scorn and shame.

antiphon—

O Lord Jesus Christ,

Burdened with your cross,

Mounting even to Calvary,

Bearing the weight of our sins.

antiphon—

O Lord Jesus Christ,

Stripped of your garments,

Given gall in your thirst,

Crucified with thieves.

antiphon—

O Lord Jesus Christ,

Forgiving your executioners,

Confiding your holy Mother

To your beloved disciple.

antiphon—

O Lord Jesus Christ,

Breathing forth your spirit

Into the hands of your Father,

Dying for all sinners

antiphon—Have mercy, O Lord, have mercy on us!

Mercy, pity, Pietá. All are there for us.

We give thanks and praise to God on this Good Friday afternoon, that on the first Good Friday afternoon, the woman who was the first disciple of Jesus was there by the cross with him when most of his other disciples had fled. There to comfort him and to receive us. There to hold his body when it was taken down from the cross.

She is here now with us, here now to present us to him when we find life burdensome and in need of the rest that only he can give.

22

Resurrection of the Lord: Easter Vigil

Death's Not What We're Moving Toward;
It's What We're Coming From!

The Gospel Reading for Year C: Luke 24:1–12

The practical conclusion to be drawn from our collective reflection on the Paschal Mystery—the mystery of Christ's death and Resurrection, the mystery of the Christian passage to life through death—is this: "Death's not what we're moving toward; it is what we're coming from!" Those are the words of Fr. Clarence Rivers, a priest-composer of liturgical music and a pioneer many years ago in bringing African-American Catholic culture to bear on contemporary liturgical celebration.

"Death's not what we're moving toward; it is what we're coming from!" The death and Resurrection of Jesus once and forever freed the entire human race from the grip of death. Death can never hold you because you have died with Christ who has been raised from the dead. This is what we celebrate in the sacrament of baptism where you are plunged (that's the meaning of the verb "baptize") into the death of Jesus so that, with Jesus you can rise and walk in newness of life. Once you are baptized, you've been raised with him. Easter celebrates his Resurrection and yours. His has happened. Yours will come. Both are intertwined in the sacrament of baptism.

St. Paul put it this way in his Letter to the Romans (6:3–4): "Are you unaware that we who were baptized into Christ Jesus were baptized into his death? We were indeed buried with him through baptism into death, so that, just as Christ was raised from the dead by the glory of the Father, we too might live in newness of life."

We too might live a new life. "Death's not what we're moving toward; it is what we're coming from."

Listen again to those angels, those messengers, "two men in dazzling garments" that the women carrying spices met when they came to the tomb. The women, you will recall from the Gospel account, "were terrified and bowed their faces to the ground. [The men in dazzling garments] said to them: 'Why do you seek the living one among the dead? He is not here, but he has been raised. Remember what he said to you while he was still in Galilee, that the Son of Man must be handed over to sinners and be crucified, and rise on the third day.' And they remembered his words."

You also must remember his words. Remember the promise of the Resurrection as we celebrate in this Easter Vigil the sacraments of baptism and confirmation. Remember the promise of the Resurrection as we make or renew our baptismal promises tonight. And let yourself thrill at the promise you have, in and through the Resurrection of Jesus, that death's not what you're moving toward, it is indeed what you've left behind in the waters of baptism.

Be grateful and praise the Lord!

V
Easter Season to
The Body and Blood of Christ

· · · · · · · · · · · · · · · ·

23

Easter Sunday

Peter Has a Vitally Important Message for You

Acts 10:34a, 37–43; Psalm 118; Colossians 3:14; John 20:1–9

The first reading in today's liturgy of the word, the first of the readings for Easter Sunday morning, is from the Acts of the Apostles. It has St. Peter speaking directly to you, so listen attentively; Peter has a vitally important message for you. "You know," says Peter,

> …what has happened all over Judea, beginning in Galilee after the baptism that John preached, how God anointed Jesus of Nazareth with the Holy Spirit and power. He went about doing good and healing all those oppressed by the devil, for God was with him. We [meaning Peter and the other disciples] are witnesses of all that he did both in the country of the Jews and in Jerusalem. They put him to death by hanging him on a tree. This man God raised up on the third day and granted that he be visible, not to all the people, but to us, the witnesses chosen by God in advance, who ate and drank with him after he rose from the dead.

This is extraordinary eyewitness testimony. Peter saw up-close and firsthand what Jesus did in the land of the Jews and in Jerusalem. He also saw the death of Jesus although he, Peter, and other close friends, cut and ran on Jesus when he was dragged off to be crucified. Peter knew firsthand of the death of Jesus on the cross. But he also knew of the Resurrection firsthand. You can "eat and drink" with someone only if that person is alive and well, actually present to you, there at table with you. Peter was there at table with Jesus after the Resurrection. Then Peter, as all of this is recorded in the Acts of the Apostles, speaks of his personal assignment, his commission. Listen again to Peter: "He commissioned us to preach to the people and testify that he is the one appointed by God to judge the living and the dead. To him all the prophets bear witness, that everyone who believes in him will receive forgiveness of sins through his name."

This is Peter's Easter message to you. Do you understand it? Do you really believe it? Peter's credentials are impeccable; you can take all this on his word. Why is it so important that you heed this message of Peter? Because, as Peter put it, "everyone who believes in him [Jesus] will receive forgiveness of sins through his name." And that, of course, applies to you!

Everything we have and are as Christians—as followers of Christ—depends on the fact of the Resurrection. If he is not risen, our faith is empty. But he did rise and Peter is testifying to that fact. His word is reassuring; his message is one we need to hear again and again. It is because we have heard this message and believe it, that we are (or should be) so deep-down grateful today; it is because the Resurrection really happened that we are different, that we are free, that we are saved.

The Gospel story today from John reminds you of the quality of Peter's credentials to be speaking to you about Easter. There he is, along with John, the younger disciple whom Jesus loved, running out to the empty tomb as if in disbelief after Mary Magdalene told them that the body of Jesus was no longer there. How could that be? They did not yet have Easter faith; didn't he tell them that he would have to face death but that he would rise again?

John outran Peter and reached the tomb first. "He bent down and saw the burial cloths there, but did not go in. When Simon Peter arrived after him, he went into the tomb and saw the burial cloths there, and the cloth that had covered the head, not with the burial cloths, but rolled up in a separate place."

Notice the courtesy of John, the younger and faster of these two disciples. He waited for Peter to catch up and let Peter enter the tomb first. The cloth that had been wrapped around the head of the dead Jesus was there, apparently rolled up by the risen Jesus himself, and set aside. The wide-eyed Peter saw all of this evidence first hand.

None of us can be untouched by the Easter message. Listen again, for instance, to the excerpt we have in today's liturgy from Paul's Letter to the Colossians: "If then you were raised with Christ, seek what is above, where Christ is seated at the right hand of God." Go ahead. Let your heart be lifted up and let your grateful self be lifted up today in the spirit of Easter joy.

No wonder we should be paying attention again to Peter on this Easter morning. This is not just another holiday or holy day; this is not just one of many religious observances. No, Easter is unique. It is Resurrection Day. Let yourself feel it in your heart this morning, an especially grateful heart on this Easter Sunday.

24

Second Sunday of Easter

Peace and Faith

Acts 5:12–16; Psalm 118; Revelation 1:9–11a, 12–13, 17–19;
John 20:19–31

"Peace be with you," Jesus says to his post-Resurrection disciples. "Peace be with you," he says to each one of you today. Peace is his gift to you. Peace is the legacy he leaves with you now that he is risen, now that he is victorious, now that he reigns with Father and Holy Spirit in eternal glory, as you remain on earth following in faith your Risen Lord. "Peace be with you."

Are you at peace today? This is not to ask, "Are you complacent, are you numb, are you tuned out, sleepwalking, disengaged?" It is rather to ask, "Are you at peace, in balance, in touch with your Risen Lord?" His victory is a victory for you. It is not so much that you have picked a winner, but that a winner—an eternal winner, the Jesus of glory—has picked you. Therefore, be at peace. Let nothing disturb you. "Peace be with you." Peace was defined by St. Thomas Aquinas as "the tranquility of right order." Are you tranquil today?

Put yourself in the midst of that band of close disciples who huddled there in the Upper Room, he showed them his hands and his side where hours earlier there was blood, but now they see not marks of torture but badges of honor, signs of victory. He will suffer no more; he is king forever.

"Peace be with you." "Then he said to Thomas, 'Put your finger here and see my hands, and bring your hand and put it into my side, and do not be unbelieving, but believe.' "

How often as a child did you repeat the singsong error, "Seeing is believing, seeing is believing?" You don't believe what you see; you know what you see. You have sensory evidence, experiential knowledge of what you see. You believe only what you cannot see. You take it to be true on the testimony of another, not on any direct sensible experience of that which is believed.

Now be assured that doubt does not disqualify you from the community of believers. We all have our doubts. But faith overcomes doubt. What did Jesus say to Thomas? "Do not be unbelieving, but believe." Thomas answered as each of you can answer out of the depths of your doubt, "My Lord and my God!"

Then Jesus spoke words to him that are really intended for you: "Have you come to believe because you have seen me? Blessed are those who have not seen and have believed."

Those words apply to each one of you. "Blessed are those who have not seen and have believed." That's you! You haven't seen the Risen Lord and yet you believe that he did indeed rise from the dead. Even if you had seen him when he walked the earth, you, like Magdalene and all his other disciples, would have to make a post-Resurrection adjustment. You would have to learn, as they did during these privileged moments when he appeared to them after rising from the tomb, that the physical contacts of the past are no longer possible. If they want to touch him now, cling to him now, follow him from now on, they would have to touch, cling, and follow with the embrace of faith. That is exactly your situation today.

So if you hesitated to say yes to my earlier inquiry about whether or not you are now at peace, or perhaps said no within the quiet confines of your heart, if you admitted to the absence of peace within your heart, perhaps you were admitting to a deficit of faith.

Believe and peace will follow. Believe and balance will come into control. Be in touch with your Risen Lord—and remember you can touch him now only by faith—be in touch with your Risen Lord and feel a marvelous peace settle into your heart.

Now you might still feel compelled to say, no, no, there is still no peace. And I can only reply, let go, let go, and simply believe; "do not be unbelieving, but believe." With Thomas, permit yourself to say now, and especially at Communion time today, "My Lord and my God!" Just say it and let the healing begin. Let the doubts diminish. For after all, if Jesus conquered death, if his Father raised him from the tomb, they together with their Holy Spirit can conquer your doubts; they can deepen your faith.

Listen to these words from the priest's prayer immediately before Communion in every Mass; this is the old translation before the latest version of the Roman Missal: "Lord Jesus Christ, Son of the living God, by the will of the Father and the work of the Holy Spirit, your death brought life to the world. By your holy body and blood free me from all my sins, and from every evil. Keep me faithful to your teaching, and never let me be parted from you."

Make that prayer your own. Give it your own Amen in Holy Communion today as you borrow the lines from the doubting Thomas and simply say, "My Lord and my God!"

"Peace be with you."

25

Third Sunday of Easter

I'm Going Fishing

Acts 5:27–32, 40b–41; Psalm 30; Revelation 5:11–14; John 21:1–19

Put yourself in the sandals of the disciples of Jesus. Recall how in this post-Resurrection period Jesus "shows up" from time to time. How would you be on the lookout for his appearances? What would you do to occupy yourself in those intervals between his appearances? Recall that you had deserted him when he was arrested. Think of how you might want to make amends. And while you are thinking, recall his post-Resurrection encounters with those who had been close to him over the previous three years.

He simply appeared to Magdalene (who, by the way, never deserted him) in the early morning and she mistook him for the gardener. He came through the doors into the Upper Room one evening, you will recall, and presented himself there to the doubting Thomas. You will also remember that he fell into step and walked along one afternoon with two of them on the road to Emmaus. That was when their hearts "burned within them" as he interpreted for them the Scriptures; they then invited him in to stay with them and eventually "recognized him in the breaking of the bread."

So, put yourself into the sandals of the post-Resurrection disciples and ask yourself what you would do—repentant for your desertion, your loss of confidence in him, your lack of faith—what would you do while awaiting your Risen Lord? You are eager and ready to work with him now in spreading the good news, in continuing his work on earth, launching the great enterprise he had come to establish. How would you occupy yourself in those in-between times when he was not physically present?

Peter shows you the way in the Gospel story you just heard from John. Peter says, "I am going fishing."

First recall that Peter had denied him three times. I have a wonderful picture of an engraving by the late Minnesota artist Joseph O'Connell. It is called *The Denial of Peter* (1969). It depicts an anguished Peter breaking the neck of the cock whose crowing amounted to a ringing indictment of Peter. In "A Meditation on Peter's Denial as Imaged by Joseph O'Connell" (*Divine Favor: The Art of Joseph O'Connell*, Liturgical Press, 1999), Mary Hynes-Berry writes:

> Isn't it just like denial?
>
> A vortex.
>
> We see the circles within circles within circles spiraling away when we falsely protest. No… It wasn't…I didn't…
>
> And afterward, when it dawns upon us what we have done, we are caught in a whirlwind of denial, crying our eyes out, we protest again.
>
> I didn't…
>
> I didn't…
>
> I didn't mean….
>
> But the dawn has already crept away from the blessed confusion of night. The authorities have come. They are leading away Him whom we know to be our best chance of salvation.
>
> No matter how heartfelt, our protest grows fainter in the ever clearer light.
>
> So we do what we can in an effort to keep from being sucked down in sorrow and guilty despair. We wring the stupid cock's neck—if he had just been quiet, it would have been alright. The darkness would have understood our fear, hidden it, forgiven us the consequences. But oh no, that rooster, preening in his role, not once, not twice, but three times trumpeted to the world the dayspring from on high. Everything is his fault we tell ourselves righteously. Crowing in triumph, he betrays our denial of denial. So, wringing his neck, wringing our hands, eyes

streaming with tears of guilty regret we stand at the center of that vortex. And yet, as faint as the dawn, we hope.

Peter had hope. You can relate to his anguished guilt. Can you also relate to his hope, his everyday hope, his in-between times hope? Let me explain.

Locate yourself on the shore of the Sea of Tiberias, also known as the Sea or Lake of Galilee. "Together were Simon Peter, Thomas called Didymus, Nathanael from Cana in Galilee, Zebedee's sons, and two others of his disciples. Simon Peter said to them, 'I am going fishing.'"

Well there you have Peter's reply to the question of how he would spend the in-between time, those uncertain intervals between the unscheduled appearances of the Risen Lord. "I am going fishing," says Peter. In effect, he is saying, "I'm going back to work." It is not recreational fishing that he's referring to. Fishing is his profession. Fishing is what he does for a living. He's making a very important statement here that is applicable to each of you today. If you want to find Jesus, you can find him in your work—in the associates and circumstances in your world of work, in the day-to-day routine of work. It is there that you can find the Lord.

Follow this Gospel story a bit closer now. The other disciples—fishermen too—decided to join Peter. "So they went out and got into the boat, but that night they caught nothing. When it was already dawn, Jesus was standing on the shore (there he is again, he just shows up unannounced!); but the disciples did not realize that it was Jesus." Unproductive labor, all night long. Hard work; no results.

"Jesus said to them, (now remember they did not know it was Jesus standing on the shore; it was just a voice coming to them over the water, and the voice first asks a question and then offers unsolicited advice!): 'Children, have you caught anything to eat?'" Jesus gets a polite monosyllabic reply: "No." Then comes the advice. Remember they were professionals and this stranger tells them, "Cast the net over the right side of the boat and you will find something." Who's the expert here? Whose pride, whose professional reputation is at stake? Who asked for any advice? Yet the Gospel account tells you that they followed the advice, cast the net on the other side, "and were not able to pull it in because of the number of fish." It was not until after the catch, after they had taken the unsolicited advice, that they recognized "It is the Lord." When Simon Peter heard those words from John, he jumped into the water and swam ashore, and the others followed dragging the great catch of fish.

The lesson? Throw yourself into your work and you will find the Lord. Persevere through the dark hours, put up with discouragement, don't give up just because there is "no catch." Stick with it and you will encounter the Lord. Moreover, just because he may be silent, never conclude that he is absent. He is there by your side (or standing off a bit on the shore.) You are there—in your particular place of work—by his providence, according to his plan. You are called by him to be there. You can find him there, in your work or wherever he might be calling you to move if it is indeed time for a change.

From time to time you will have a special sense of his presence and his power in your regard. You will participate in some fashion in a miraculous catch. You will be privileged from time to time to "breakfast with him," as his disciples did on the lakeshore.

There will be times when he speaks to you by name, as he spoke to Peter, and he will ask: "Do you love me?" That question could come your way at Communion time today. You like Peter will protest (at least three times—making up for the triple denial?) that you do indeed love him. He will ask you to feed his lambs and care for his sheep. Isn't it great to know that you can do just that through meeting your nine-to-five, Monday-through-Friday workplace responsibilities? When you meet your workplace responsibilities, you can also meet the Lord, just as Peter did.

26

Fourth Sunday of Easter

Reassurance from the Good Shepherd

Acts 13:14, 43–52; Psalm 100; Revelation 7:9, 14b–17; John 10:27–30

These are reassuring readings, these texts that you just heard from Sacred Scripture. They speak of security and salvation. They use imagery of sheep and shepherd. And in the Gospel reading—a very short "Good Shepherd" segment from the Gospel of John—you hear Jesus say to and of you: "I give them eternal life, and they shall never perish. No one can take them out of my hand."

Are you uncomfortable in applying those words to yourself? You should certainly not be complacent in the assurance you have here that Jesus knows you, as a shepherd knows his sheep; that Jesus holds you in his hand, as the Good Shepherd is so often pictured holding the lost sheep and carrying it back to the fold; that Jesus gives you eternal life and that you will "never perish." As I say, you should not be complacent about all this, but neither should you be uncomfortable in applying these words to yourself.

Curiously, we tend to resist these reassurances. We tend to fend off—at least from ourselves—the assertion that we are good, the assurances we have that we are, by God's grace, saved. Others maybe, yes; but me? I'm not so sure. Well, you can be sure—that's what faith is all about. And you can be sure without being presumptuous. You know you have work to do, and you accept that fact. You know that you are not worthy, but you also know that you are graced and gifted beyond all imagining, and, despite your unworthiness, you will have eternal life. There is no snatching you out of the hand of your Lord, your Good Shepherd.

All you can be is grateful. And grateful you must be. That's why you are here before the altar today. That's why you come here every Sunday. You are here to give praise and thanks to God for your gift of salvation in Christ Jesus. It is an unmerited gift, but it is yours nonetheless. All you can be is grateful!

Go back to the first reading—the one from the Acts of the Apostles—and see Paul and Barnabas on their missionary journey to Antioch in Pisidia. They sat down in the synagogue and urged their hearers to "remain faithful to the grace of God." On the following Sabbath, almost the entire city turned out to listen to them. They proclaimed the good news to the Gentiles. The Book of Acts says: "The Gentiles were delighted when they heard this and glorified the word of the Lord. All who were destined for eternal life came to believe, and the word of the Lord continued to spread."

The word of the Lord comes down to you again today. Like the disciples of Paul and Barnabas, you should, as the Book of Acts puts it, be "filled with joy and the Holy Spirit."

"We are his people, the sheep of his flock," is the way the responsorial psalm puts it. And so you are! And as the selection you heard from the Book of Revelation puts it, again speaking of you, "For the Lamb who is in the center of the throne will shepherd them and lead them to springs of life-giving water, and God will wipe away every tear from their eyes." Pray for the grace to let these reassuring words sink in, to penetrate your souls today, to lift your hearts, transform your outlook, fill you with peace.

Again, this is no time for complacency and certainly not for presumption. But God's grace is at work in you. It is powerful; it can overcome the world. It can certainly displace your doubts. Let your faith move you now to entrust yourself to God, to place you into the arms of the Good Shepherd. This is the same Good Shepherd who waits to embrace you in the sacrament of reconciliation, who nourishes you in the Eucharist, who speaks to you in Scripture. Of course, you are weak and unworthy, but you are strengthened by his forgiveness; you've been made strong in all your broken places. Don't permit the enemy of your human nature—Satan—to convince you otherwise. You and I are fair game for temptations to self-doubt, even to self-hatred. We need the grace and reassuring words that our Good Shepherd brings; we need the sense of security that his embrace can give.

"My sheep hear my voice; I know them, and they follow me. I give them eternal life, and they shall never perish. No one can take them out of my hand. My Father, who has given them to me, is greater than all, and no one can take them out of the Father's hand. The Father and I are one."

You don't have to take any of this on my word; just listen and let him speak for himself.

27

Fifth Sunday of Easter

"Behold, I Make All Things New"

Acts 14:21–27; Psalm 145; Revelation 21:1–5; John 13:31–35

Instead of reflecting with you this morning on the New Commandment of love, articulated by Jesus in the Gospel reading, I want to lift a single line from the second reading—the Book of Revelation—and post it as a banner for celebration, a motto for repetition, and a divinely inspired exclamation intended to give you hope. I refer, of course, to the words: "Behold, I make all things new."

"I make all things new."

Hear those words and try to enjoy a hope-filled vision. There are many visions in the Book of Revelation. I make no claim to expert understanding of this last book of the Bible; I don't even claim competence in interpreting it. It is a very difficult book to understand—so much symbolism, so many numbers and strange assertions. But it is nonetheless a part of our Bible and—this much I know—it is intended to give us hope.

The victory of Jesus over Satan is certain. The victory has been won. Your belief in Jesus, and your commitment to him, put you in the winner's circle. You can and should experience within your heart a surge of hope—hope that will last. That's what this Book of Revelation is telling you. That's why, I think, the Church puts these words before you in this liturgy for the Fifth Sunday of Easter.

So it is a good thing, a healthy exercise, here on the Fifth Sunday of Easter to try to catch a glimpse of the vision of victory. Who is it, in the Book of Revelation, who says, "Behold, I make all things new"? It is God speaking, revealing himself in Christ, and promising to "dwell" with you, to wipe every tear from your eyes, to do away with death and mourning and pain, and thus to make all things new. That is certainly

going to happen. That day is coming. So try to see it now, try to antici-
pate it, and with that vision welcome hope into your heart.

God never intended that you live without hope. There may be many
deprivations in your life—there will be pain, mourning, even death—
but you must never deprive yourself of hope.

It is said that this twenty-first chapter from the Book of Revelation
was Emily Dickinson's favorite Scripture passage. With the poet's eye,
she could catch the vision God invites us all to grasp. With her poet's
mind, she could understand and later write: "I dwell in Possibility—"

You can "dwell in possibility" if your heart is full of hope. And both
faithful and hopeful, as you are, in your vocation to follow Christ, you
should look around you at the city you now inhabit, recognizing that
God dwells here with you, and you should ask yourself, what might I
do to improve this city for all its inhabitants? What might I be doing
now to make this city new? Catch the confidence of the God who says,
"Behold, I make all things new," and make yourself available to work
along with him—to the extent that you can—to make your city new.
You can renew it intellectually and spiritually, perhaps; maybe you can
enhance the physical environment. No reason why you cannot attempt
to expand the supply of kindness and care in your city, thus making
God more fully present here.

You dwell in possibility. And the possibilities for improvement within you and around you are virtually infinite.

Another poet, Elizabeth Barrett Browning, found inspiration in the
Book of Exodus (3:1–14) where an angel of the Lord appearing to
Moses in "fire flaming out of a bush." The bush, although on fire, was
not consumed.

So Moses decided to walk over to the bush and take a closer look.
The Scripture passage tells you, "When the Lord saw that he had turned
aside to look, God called out to him from the bush: Moses! Moses!" It
is God's voice, not the angel's that calls from inside the burning bush.
God calls Moses by name. And Moses says, "Here I am."

"God said, 'Do not come near! Remove the sandals from your feet,
for the place where you stand is holy ground. I am the God of your
fathers,' he continued, 'the God of Abraham, the God of Isaac, the

God of Jacob.'" Moses "hid his face," the Scripture tells us, "for he was afraid to look at God."

Then, as you remember, God told Moses that he was there to rescue his chosen people from the hands of the Egyptians and to lead them out of bondage into a land "flowing with milk and honey." Moses, you will recall, asked God how, when he, Moses, went to the Israelites, he should identify God, what name would he give them. "God replied to Moses: 'I am who I am....This is what you shall tell the Israelites: 'I AM sent me to you.' This is my name forever; this is my title for all generations."

Well here we are—our generation, just one in the flow of so many generations—and this is how we should name and think of our God, as "I AM."

God is in our midst. Somehow or other we should be able to seek and find God in all things. God is in us, and around us, in front of us, behind us, beside us. There are "burning bushes" around us and we must take care that we not just walk by without noticing God, without "seeing" or "hearing" God present to us in our world.

Perhaps you have not remembered your God that way, as existence, as present in you and all around you. Perhaps reflection on these readings this morning will awaken you, will bring you, so to speak, to your senses—your spiritual sense of sight, to sharpen your vision to the presence of God. You too will then see your way more clearly to work with God in making "all things new."

28

Sixth Sunday of Easter

"Peace I Leave with You; My Peace I Give to You"

Acts 15:1–2, 22–29; Psalm 67; Revelation 21:10–14, 22–23;
John 14:23–29

"Jesus said to his disciples...Peace I leave with you; my peace I give to you. Not as the world gives do I give it to you."

"'Peace! Peace!'...though there is no peace," said the Lord through the prophet Jeremiah some 2,600 years ago. How many times through the centuries have we thought we had peace between nations only to find it eluding us? "'Peace! Peace!'...though there is no peace." How many times in how many lives over the centuries have men and women dreamed of finding peace of heart, and how few times and in how few lives has true peace of heart been achieved?

Yet here we have the promise, the legacy of peace given to us by Jesus: "Peace I leave with you; my peace I give to you. Not as the world gives [peace] do I give it to you. Do not let your hearts be troubled or afraid."

How does the world give peace? Negotiated settlements. Cease-fires. Truces. It is always a compromise, always less than perfect. "Piecemeal peace is poor peace," wrote the poet Gerard Manley Hopkins ("Peace," 1918).

The world gives its piecemeal peace grudgingly, reluctantly, suspiciously, tentatively. One hand reaches out; the other remains ready to strike. One hand pretends to give; the other prepares to take. That's why voices down through the centuries in all parts of the world (and within our own troubled hearts) keep repeating: "'Peace! Peace!'...though there is no peace,." You can study that sixth chapter in the Book of Jeremiah to search for a few clues that help explain why peace eluded the Israelites and remains for so many today out of reach: "For

I will stretch forth my hand against those who dwell in this land," says the Lord. "Small and great alike, all are greedy for gain; prophet and priest, all practice fraud…They have acted shamefully, committing abominations, yet they are not at all ashamed, they know not how to blush…Thus says the LORD: Stand by the earliest roads, ask the pathways of old, 'Which is the way to good?' and walk it; thus you will find rest for your selves" (Jer 6:12–16).

"Greedy for gain." Have you noticed that—nationally or personally, in yourself or others?

"Fraud"? Any signs of that in the news, in the workplace, in yourself? Have you noticed anything "odious" in human affairs, anything "abominable," anything in daily life, in inner-, outer-, or cyber-space that should prompt shame and make a normal, healthy person blush? If we live beyond the reach of shame, we will not achieve peace of heart.

What is peace, anyway? St. Thomas Aquinas defined it as the "tranquility of right order." That suggests the wisdom of getting your act together, tidying up your life as a means of finding personal peace. It includes, of course, the wisdom of righting your relationships with God. It also suggests the necessity of public order, of just relations between nations, if peace is to reign in international relations. Peace has to be a lot more than whatever it is that follows a truce or cease-fire. Settlement of a dispute is not a guarantee of peace. Peace has something to do with abiding balance—balance in a human life, balance between the interests of employers and employees, between organizations and between nations. There can be no peace without balance (whether it is a balance of payments, of interests, of power in public affairs; a balance of values, appetites, and commitments in personal affairs). And, of course, there can be no peace without the great balancing factor of love.

Recall what the Lord said through the prophet Jeremiah: "Stand by the earliest roads (in other words, go back to basic principles, return to the old truths, to your solid core values), ask the pathways of old: 'Which is the way to good?' and walk it; thus you will find rest for your selves." Rest for your souls means peace.

Once you locate those "pathways of old," which are the "way to good," you have to walk accordingly. You've got choices to make, values to adopt, principles to internalize.

Take a moment or two today to run an inventory check on your values, your basic principles. Are they the right ones to keep you on the road to peace? Take a look at our nation's values. Are they the right ones to keep us as a nation on the road to peace? If not, what can you do to change them?

There is a famous prayer attributed to St. Francis of Assisi. You've heard it and prayed it often. Review it now as a blueprint, a strategy for peace.

Lord, make me an instrument of your peace.

Where there is hatred, let me sow love.

Where there is injury, pardon.

Where there is discord, unity.

Where there is doubt, faith.

Where there is error, truth.

Where there is despair, hope.

Where there is sadness, joy.

Where there is darkness, light.

O Divine Master,

grant that I may not so much seek to be consoled, as to console;

to be understood, as to understand;

to be loved, as to love.

For it is in giving that we receive.

It is in pardoning that we are pardoned.

It is in dying that we are born to eternal life.

Comb through those words to come up with the elements of a working strategy for peace —personal peace or peace between any opposing parties, nations, and organizations. What do you come up with? Love, pardon, unity, faith, truth, hope, joy. How strategically important is it for you personally and for any opposing parties to seek not so much "to be understood as to understand"?

Peace, peace, and there is no peace. Why? Because this strategy has not yet been tried. "Peace I leave with you; my peace I give to you. Not as the world gives do I give [peace] to you. Do not let your hearts be troubled or afraid."

Be not afraid. How often did Jesus say those reassuring words in his post-Resurrection appearances! Hear him say those words to you today. Be not afraid to do what must be done for your personal reception and assimilation of the gift of peace.

29

Ascension

"Why Are You Standing There Looking at the Sky?"

Acts 1:1–11; Psalm 47; Ephesians 1:17–23; Luke 24:46–53

"Why are you standing there looking at the sky?" ask the two angels speaking to the apostles from whose midst Jesus was "taken up…into heaven." That is how it is recorded in the Acts of the Apostles; you heard the account in today's first reading. Apply that question to your-selves on this day when we celebrate the Feast of the Ascension: "Why are you standing there," so to speak, "looking at the sky?"

This is a biblical injunction against looking up, against trying to find Christ in the heavens instead of looking for him in your immediate surroundings, in your neighbors, in yourself, in your work and family. "Why are you standing or sitting there looking at the sky?" Come down to earth, this angelic message advises you. Keep your feet planted on the ground. Don't be idly looking up. Nor should you be looking back with regret. The only direction for your vision in this post-Resurrection, post-Ascension world is straight ahead. Look straight ahead into an unknown future where the Risen Christ awaits you, into which the Risen Christ invites you, and through which the Christ of glory will accompany you.

Don't look up. Don't look back. Look straight ahead with the eye of faith.

I have two points for your consideration today by way of reflec-tion on these Ascension readings. The first is power. The second is Ascension hope.

First power. I would not expect you to do a frequency count of the number of times the word power occurred in today's readings. But you may have noticed it occurring. By my count it comes up four times.

In the selection from the Acts of the Apostles, you heard the Lord's promise to his apostles (and to you) that "you will receive power when the Holy Spirit comes upon you, and you will be my witnesses in Jerusalem, throughout Judea and Samaria, and to the ends of the earth." That means even to the zip code where you now reside!

In the second reading taken from Paul's Letter to the Ephesians, "power" occurs twice: Paul wants you to know "what is the surpassing greatness of his [God's] power for us who believe." And later, how God raised Christ above every [earthly] "principality, authority, power, and dominion."

And in the Gospel of Matthew (read in Year A), Jesus approached the eleven disciples and "said to them, 'All power in heaven and on earth has been given to me...And behold, I am with you always, until the end of the age." Until the end of the world, including right now! This power is yours, in Christ, right now.

You understand power best when you think of it as relational, not as something fixed in place—heavy, immovable, impenetrable. You are empowering me at the moment to speak. If you were to get up and leave, if you withdrew this empowering relationship, there would be no one here to listen and therefore no point at all in my speaking. You empower me.

Your relationship to the post-Resurrection, post-Ascension Christ, to the Jesus of glory, empowers you with the power that is his. Through you, his power touches your world, your workplace, your family, your neighborhood. All you need do is choose to be faithful to him, to maintain your relationship of fidelity. He is with you, and with his Church, always, and that includes you so long as you do what is required of you to maintain the relationship; in other words, so long as you want him there, so long as you choose to remain faithful. He doesn't ask you to be strong or brilliant; he simply asks that you be faithful and in your fidelity you will find power, his power made available to you. He empowers you.

This brings us to our second point: Ascension hope. Hope is a theological virtue and that simply means that its object is God. You hope not in yourself, nor in your treasure, your intelligence, nor your possessions. Your ultimate hope and the ground of your being is God.

Listen again to Paul's words to the Ephesians—you heard these words in the second reading: "May the eyes of [your] hearts be enlightened, that you may know what is the hope that belongs to his call." Pray, dear friends, that the eyes of your hearts may be enlightened today as we celebrate the Feast of the Ascension. Pray for hope. Pray for the hope that is "his call."

We don't always carry a full supply of hope. But we should remember that hope is no virtue at all unless things are really hopeless! It is when there seems to be no hope at all emerging from our own resources that we come to the enlightened realization that all hope comes from God (it is "his call" to us). Moreover, our hope is God revealed to us in his glorified Christ, the Christ whose Ascension we celebrate today.

The eleven disciples gathered there with Jesus on the mount of the Ascension still had doubts. Now this was after several post-Resurrection appearances of the Lord to them. Maybe you have doubts. You worship, but you have your doubts. Just try to remember that Jesus said to his disciples and to you: "I am with you always, until the end of the age.'"

Great words. Reassuring words. Let this day be a day of love and gratitude to God for his gift to you in the risen and ascended Christ. Be grateful. And be ready to rise with him, as he promised you, on the last day.

30

Seventh Sunday of Easter

Christian Unity: "That They May All Be One"

Acts 7:55–60; Psalm 97; Revelation 22:12–14, 16–17, 20;
John 17:20–26

Listen carefully once again to these words from today's Gospel and notice that they indicate that Jesus said this prayer specifically for you: "Jesus prayed, saying: 'Holy Father, I pray not only for them [his apostles], but also for those who will believe in me through their word.'" That means you, individually and collectively—you are one of those that he knew then would come in future times to believe in him through the testimony and words of the apostles.

Think about that. Jesus had you in mind—prayed for you—when he offered this prayer to his Father: "...that they may all be one, as you, Father, are in me and I in you, that they also may be in us, that the world may believe that you sent me." Now notice again, when he prayed for our unity, he did so in order that "the world may believe." In other words, the spectacle of our Christian unity would convince those who observed our unity that Christ, the principle and focus of our unity, was indeed sent by God. And they too then would become Christians.

This phrase from the high-priestly prayer of Jesus—"that they may be one"—was the theme for the pontificate of the great Pope John XXIII, whose enthusiasm for Christian unity permeated the Second Vatican Council and launched the modern ecumenical movement, a movement meant to promote Christian unity, not simply to encourage tolerance and interfaith understanding. So pray today in the spirit of John XXIII and in the words of Jesus, "that they may all be one," and remember that the unity we pray for has the witness value of drawing "the world" to believe in Jesus.

How far we are today, twenty centuries after Jesus first prayed those words, how far we are from Christian unity! Think of all our divisions and divides, and think of what we might do to close those gaps. But let me caution you against undue surprise or discouragement over difference and divisions in your life—your personal life or your lives as denominationally divided Christians. Listen to the late Henri de Lubac, SJ, on this point:

To differ, even deeply, from one another, is not to be enemies; it is simply to be. To recognize and accept one's own difference is not pride. To recognize and accept the difference of others is not weakness. If union has to be, if union offers any meaning at all, it must be union between different people. And it is above all in the recognition and acceptance of difference that difference is overcome and union achieved. (*Further Paradoxes*)

There is a lot of wisdom in those words, particularly with respect to differences between persons. But they apply as well to religious differences and divides. So do not lose heart. Do not be scandalized by the differences. Just continue to pray the high-priestly prayer of Jesus, "that they may all be one." And do something practical from time to time to help make this unity happen.

Tolerance and interfaith understanding are important first steps, of course. I always like the motto of the Gustave Weigel Society, an ecumenical group of Christian clergy in the Washington, DC, area back in the 1960s: "Knowledge and love first; unity later." Knowledge and love are, in this context, like knowledge and developing love in a courtship, a preamble to genuine unity. So a good first step is to expand our knowledge of and cultivate our love for persons of other faith communities.

On Pentecost Sunday, we celebrate the coming of the Holy Spirit to all of us. It would be great if we could offer a visible sign of continuing steps among Christians toward unity, toward full communion, by walking with Christians of neighboring churches and praying with them for unity.

Let's reflect for a few minutes now on unity. There is only one God. God is truly unique. Our unique God is the principle and source of our unity. Our unique God is Triune—Father, Son, and Holy Spirit. There is a Trinitarian basis for our unity in Christ, formed as we are into the one Body of Christ by the will of God and by the work of the Holy Spirit.

For us, there are three essential elements of unity: faith, worship, and service. God revealed himself to us as Triune. We believe (that's our faith). We meet and worship our God in the sacraments, especially in the Eucharist (the sacrament of unity). We show our love for one another in service. Faith, worship, service. All three require commitments that we freely give, and in giving worship and service, we receive fuller shares of the unmerited gift of faith. All we can really give to God is thanks. That's what Eucharist means!

Now a word about the so-called ecumenical movement. This refers to the initiatives and activities that encourage Christian unity. The goal? "That they may be one." In and through the ecumenical movement our Church commits itself to spiritual renewal, theological dialogue and a common mission of witnessing to unity through service (and, in the process, strengthening the unity to which the service gives witness).

We've got a long, long way to go. We contemporary Roman Catholics have a lot to learn from other Christians as well as from other faith communities. Under the guidance of the Holy Spirit, we can gain from the ecumenical exchange fresh insights and new experiences that deepen our Catholic faith on the way to unity. "Knowledge and love first, unity later."

Let me conclude by quoting these words from an article on ecumenism in *The New Dictionary of Theology* (1987):

The central element in Roman Catholic developments towards an ecclesiology [i.e., a theological understanding of the nature of the Church] appropriate to the ecumenical movement is a Trinitarian, Christocentric spirituality in which the focus in on Jesus Christ and the action of the Holy Spirit, and which is open to God's direction of the pilgrim people in history. Recognizing the mystery of the risen Christ in the world as a larger than Roman Catholic experience at this moment in history leaves Catholic Christians open to enhancing their own identity by ecumenical dialogue and by the evolution that will be necessary within the Catholic Church to remain faithful to its call to be the sacrament of Christ in the world for the sake of the human community. (Jeffrey Gros, FSC, *New Dictionary of Theology*, 322)

Another way of looking at this reality is to recognize that Christianity is a movement, not a monument. The Spirit is always moving and so too is the Church, which is, as you know, the people of God. Let the Spirit carry you along in a Godward and heavenward direction in the movement that is your sure and certain faith.

31

Vigil of Pentecost

"Let Anyone Who Thirsts Come to Me and Drink"

Genesis 11:1–9 (or others); Psalm 104; Romans 8:22–27;
John 7:37–39

This is the Vigil of Pentecost, the celebratory anticipation of the coming of the Holy Spirit. Jesus sets the tone of the celebration for you with a simple statement recorded in the Gospel of John: "Let anyone who thirsts come to me and drink." And he draws upon Scripture to employ a metaphor that points to the coming of the Holy Spirit. Jesus says, "As Scripture says: 'Rivers of living water will flow from within him.'"

Living water is clear, running, sparkling, vibrant water. It suggests energy and power. It is a metaphor employed by Jesus to tell you what God the Holy Spirit is like. John's Gospel account continues with this parenthetical comment: "He said this in reference to the Spirit that those who came to believe in him were to receive. There was, of course, no Spirit as yet, because Jesus had not yet been glorified." Surely there was a Spirit then, you might find yourself thinking. The Holy Spirit, the Third Person of the Holy Trinity has no beginning or end. The Spirit exists, as do the Father and the Word, from all eternity. The Spirit existed then as Jesus was speaking. Why would the evangelist John say here, "There was, of course, no Spirit as yet"?

Well, in the economy of salvation, God decreed from all eternity that the Word, the Second Person of the Trinity, would take on flesh, would become man so that he could live among us, teach us, and, according to divine plan, suffer and die for us. When he died and rose again to glory, he would hand over to us—pour within us, so to speak—the Holy Spirit, the Spirit of love between him and the Father. We would receive the Spirit of supernatural life—life eternal—whereby we could live with God forever. This is the gift of the Holy Spirit. Jesus is saying that this gift would be there for the taking by anyone who believed in him. Open yourself up through an act of faith in Jesus and you can welcome the gift of the Spirit poured, like living water, into you. That is the realized "yet" of the Pentecost moment. It happened. It happened to you and for you, and so you celebrate at this hour!

"Let anyone who thirsts come to me," said Jesus. Don't we all thirst? Is not a thirsting, a quiet questing or searching, part of the human experience? Recall that St. Augustine once said perceptively and prayerfully words that describe the human condition, words that you may want to repeat prayerfully today: "You have made us for yourself, O Lord, and our hearts are restless until they rest in you." Do those words match your own personal experience?

Haven't you experienced a certain restlessness, a kind of thirstiness? Don't you participate in a search for purpose? Aren't you always questing to some extent, searching, stretching, reaching out from within your soul? You know the restlessness that Augustine referred to.

Can't you see evidence of that restlessness in the world around you today? We always seem to be "on the road." We are constantly occupied with the "busyness" of life. The rush of things leaves us not only with unfinished projects, but unfinished thoughts! Many of us are like the kid with a guitar heading off to Nashville or—as that kid might say—"wherever." Millions in the world around us let their undefined "thirst" take them to the dry wells of materialism and sensuality. We go on looking, searching, thinking, thirsting. So in this Pentecost liturgy, slow down, stop, and hear Jesus say to you: "Let anyone who is thirsty— and I'm speaking to you, Jack, George, Mary Ann, and Betty—if you are thirsty come to me and drink, you who believe in me." Drink that living water who is the Holy Spirit whom you have within you now at this moment, even though you may not have adverted to the fact of the Spirit's presence in your distracted restlessness. That restlessness is part of the human condition. The gift of the Holy Spirit is the divine solution to that problem.

Make an act of faith in your giftedness, in the presence of the life-giving, energizing, power-providing Spirit within you.

32

Pentecost Sunday

Holy Spirit Day

Acts 2:1–11; Psalm 104; 1 Corinthians 12:3b–7, 12–13;
John 20:19–23

Today is Holy Spirit Day. We call it Pentecost because it has been fifty days since Easter. *Pente* is the Greek word for "five," and *pentekostos* means "fiftieth." The number is significant, but this is not a day about arithmetic and numbers. It is a day about the Holy Spirit of God coming to us and dwelling within us. It is a day to think of the fire of God's Holy Spirit dwelling within us.

In today's first reading, a selection from the Acts of the Apostles, you heard the words: "When the time for Pentecost was fulfilled, they were all in one place together. And suddenly there came from the sky a noise like a strong driving wind, and it filled the entire house in which they were. Then there appeared to them tongues as of fire, which parted and came to rest on each one of them. And they were all filled with the Holy Spirit...." The Holy Spirit, the Third Person of the Holy Trinity, is like a wind, like a flame. Like a strong wind or a gentle breeze, the Spirit can be present to you. Like fire, the Spirit can bring you light and warmth. "Come, Holy Spirit, fill the hearts of the faithful and kindle in them the fire of your love." "Lord, send out your Spirit, and renew the face of the earth." Each one of you today, all of us together, can be filled with the Holy Spirit. We can be fired up and ready to renew the face of the earth. At least we can be fired up to renew our small portion of the earth with love.

Sacred Scripture is telling you today that God is like a strong wind. Scripture is also saying that God is like a flickering flame. Today's texts tell you that God is like love that can be seen with the inner eye and felt in the heart. God wants to fill your heart today with the fire of his love.

In the reading from First Corinthians you were reminded that "There are different kinds of spiritual gifts but the same Spirit." "[A]nd we were all given to drink of one Spirit." There's another way to think about God the Holy Spirit. We can drink in the Holy Spirit and become refreshed, recommitted, rededicated, and ready to renew the face of the earth.

In the Gospel selection from John, you heard Jesus say, "Peace be with you." Hear him say those words to you today and take him at his word. "Peace be with you!" Be at peace therefore. Be joyful today as the apostles were then on the first Pentecost when Jesus stood in their midst and greeted them. "The disciples rejoiced when they saw the Lord" and "[Jesus] said to them again, 'Peace be with you.' " As if to offer a warranty or a guarantee with that wish, Jesus said to them (and he says today to you), "Receive the Holy Spirit."

This Holy Spirit, whose coming upon us we celebrate on this day, Pentecost Sunday, this Holy Spirit brings gifts—you've all heard of the gifts of the Holy Spirit: wisdom, understanding, knowledge, counsel (or right judgment), fortitude (which is the courage all of us need), piety (understood as a mature and proper reverence), and the last on this list of gifts is what is called "fear of the Lord," meaning a certain sense of wonder and awe. These are the gifts of Pentecost, confirmation gifts bestowed on the *confirmandi*, these are the gifts we celebrate today. These gifts enable us to work along with God in our own day for the salvation of our world. These gifts are the outpouring of God's love. The Holy Spirit is the mystery of God's love in our world.

If you ever ask yourself the question, "What is God like?" you ultimately come up with the answer that God is love. That is what all the fuss is about on Pentecost, that is what we're celebrating—the fact that God is love and that God's love is poured into us, God's love fires us up to do good things in this world, God's love warms our hearts. Just as human love on earth leads to the union of earthly humans, God's love in us unites all of us in one body, the body of Christ, the Church.

God is love. We celebrate God's gift of love to us on this Pentecost Sunday.

We all need a measure of joy that only God can give. Christ promised to be with us always, even until the end of time. He is with us now. His being with us means joy and love, wind in our sails, fire in our bellies, warmth in our hearts. It means commitment and conviction poured into the very depths of our being. Christ's being with us means forgiveness of our sins and stupidity. Christ's being with us means that each of us has at hand a generous supply of the confirmation gifts he offered to his original disciples, the gift of the Holy Spirit who, in turn, brings gifts of wisdom, understanding, knowledge, counsel, fortitude, piety, and fear of the Lord.

Choose any one of these gifts that you like to occupy your time today. Choose them all, if you like, and delight in the enhancements they bring to you. But whatever you do, choose to dwell today on the great gift of fortitude. "[T]ake courage; be stouthearted," says the psalmist (Ps 27). With the gift of fortitude, courage is yours to face the stress, sadness, anger, disappointment, and confusion that may beset you in these troubled days.

But don't just think of yourself—your confusion, doubts, anger, and your fear perhaps for the future of the Church—think of your mission. After giving them the Spirit and expressing the wish that peace would be with them, Jesus said to his disciples (as he says to you today), "As the Father has sent me, so I send you."

Consider yourself sent—sent out with a smile, with fire in your heart, with the wind of God's love at your back—consider yourself sent to bring the Spirit of Pentecost to the world beneath your feet, to a world in need of hope and help.

33

Sunday after Pentecost: Trinity Sunday

The Most Holy Trinity

Proverbs 8:22–31; Psalm 8; Romans 5:1–5; John 16:12–15

This is the Feast of the Most Holy Trinity. Let me build this Holy Trinity homily on a poem entitled "Trinity Sunday," written by the famous English poet George Herbert, who died in 1633 and who was throughout his adult life a country pastor.

Lord, who has form'd me out of mud,

And who hast redeemed me through thy blood,

And sanctified me to do good;

Purge all my sins done heretofore:

For I confess my heavy score,

And I will strive to sin no more.

Enrich my heart, mouth, hands in me,

With faith, with hope, with charity;

That I may run, rise, rest with thee.

Creator, Redeemer, Sanctifier—the one God in three persons. Creator, Redeemer, Sanctifier—the Blessed Trinity, three divine persons constituting our one God.

Creator: "Lord, who has formed me out of mud."

Redeemer: "And who hast redeemed me through thy blood."

Sanctifier: "And sanctified me to do good."

And the poet continues in his third stanza with three little "trinities," or threesomes, or triplets of petitions that apply to each one of you:

> Enrich my heart, mouth, hands in me,
>
> With faith, with hope, with charity;
>
> That I may run, rise, rest with thee.

How might you give a Trinitarian response to the mystery of the Most Holy Trinity in your life, dear friends? First, commit yourself to God's service. Commit your whole self—heart, mouth, hands—to God wherever you are, in whatever state and stage of life God's providence has placed you.

Your heart: Does God have a place in your deepest longings, in your affections, in your human love? Where, if you will only allow it, is God's love drawing your heart right now? Is there any distance now between your heart and the heart of God?

Your mouth: Do you speak like a Christian, like a follower of Christ? Or does your speech betray you and convict you of convictions that are not of God, far from God, opposed to God?

Your hands: What are you doing for God? What have you done for God? What might you do for God in the days, months, and years ahead?

What is your triple response—heart, mouth, hands—to the call of the Most Holy Trinity?

The poet would have you pray to be enriched "with faith, with hope, with charity"—the three-part treasury that is yours by the grace of your Triune God. Faith, the act by which you entrust yourself to God; hope, the conviction that sustains you when things appear to be hopeless; charity, the love that knows no petty perimeter but reaches far beyond your own self-interest and stretches home to God. Your faith, hope, and charity—the single object of all three is your Triune God in whom you believe, in whom you hope, and to whom you offer your love today. Father, Son, and Holy Spirit, the Creator, Redeemer, and Sanctifier, who formed you "out of mud," redeemed you "though [his] blood," and sanctified you "to do good." What good might you consider doing now? Talk it over with your Triune God on this Trinity Sunday.

With your heart, mouth, and hands enriched, as they by God's good grace now are enriched with faith, hope, and charity, you are ready to "run, rise, and rest" with God.

Run, rise, and rest. Where? To what purpose? What do those verbs stir up in your imaginations? What do they invite you to be or to become? If you failed in the past to run (and hardly ever even walked along the path God's will invited you to traverse); if you chose not to rise to divine initiatives in the past, but preferred to sink instead into sinful self-centeredness; if you could not rest with God but scurried restlessly instead through life up until now, then the second stanza of George Herbert's "Trinity Sunday" poem is right for you:

> Purge all my sins done heretofore:
>
> For I confess my heavy score,
>
> And I will strive to sin no more.

Could the Triune God be anything but pleased to hear those words from you on this Trinity Sunday? Repeat them to the extent that they apply and prepare yourself for three- and thirty-fold forgiveness and an abundance of love from your Triune God—Father, Son, and Holy Spirit—who is with you now and promises to remain with you forever.

And so we pray:

> Lord, who has form'd me out of mud,
>
> And who hast redeemed me through thy blood,
>
> And sanctified me to do good;
>
> Purge all my sins done heretofore:

For I confess my heavy score,

And I will strive to sin no more.

Enrich my heart, mouth, hands in me,

With faith, with hope, with charity;

That I may run, rise, rest with thee.

May abundant blessings be yours this Trinity Sunday!

34

The Body and Blood of Christ

The Bread of Life and the Bread for Life

Genesis 14:18–20; Psalm 110; 1 Corinthians 11:23–26; Luke 9:11–17

As we pause to reflect on the relevance for us today of this ancient story of the miraculous multiplication of the loaves and fishes by our Lord Jesus Christ during the days he walked this earth, let me offer, by way of pre-note, this fact about hunger in our world today: At this very moment, as a result of the global financial problems along with war, drought, political instability, high food prices, and widespread poverty, one billion people are, by United Nations estimates, numbered in the ranks of the hungry poor. One billion. These are people who consume fewer than 1,800 calories a day. One billion of our brothers and sisters in the human community are hungry, seriously hungry, at this moment.

So keep them in your hearts, minds, and prayers as we gather here this morning to share the bread of life, the Eucharist, as we do each Sunday, at the table of the Lord. Consider for a moment what we might do when we leave here, in however small a way, to share the bread *for* life with the hungry poor in our city and around the world. We live in a world that, sad to say, is broken by unshared bread. Something can and must be done.

The texts today provide us with an opportunity to talk about hunger—world hunger, chronic malnutrition—the kind of hunger that most of us will never know, but all of us can, if we determine to do it, help eliminate. Persons like you and me who have food, may have many problems. But a person who has no food has only one problem: hunger. Despite our many problems, we can, if we choose, address that one problem and eventually eliminate hunger from the face of the earth.

According to a saying that used to make the rounds in Dorothy Day's Catholic Worker movement, "the trouble with the world is that the people who do all the thinking never act, and the people who do all the acting never think." What is particularly necessary in the face of worldwide hunger and poverty is a combination of thought and action powerful enough to deal with huge societal problems. Where faith and works combine to shape both thought and action, provisioning strategies for the hungry poor of the world will emerge. Perhaps it will not happen in the way the solution you heard in today's Gospel story occurred, where Jesus took the loaves and fish and miraculously multiplied them so that everyone had enough to eat. Don't expect that to happen today.

As you noticed, the disciples of Jesus in this story did not know what to do. So he intervened with a miracle. The disciples did not know what to do. The same might be said of us today—disciples of Christ confronted with the problem of world hunger, but not knowing what to do.

Unless you are content simply to blame the victim, you have to look around for what might be causing the physical and emotional weariness of those who suffer hunger and poverty. If the causes remain unattended, the weariness and hunger will persist and the burdens will just grow heavier. Hunger is the most urgent form of poverty, and poverty can be defined simply as sustained deprivation. The question then, of course, is deprived of what? And sustained by what? Or by whom? Poverty is the root cause of hunger. What is sustaining the poverty, which, in turn, sustains the hunger?

The poor can't count on miracles. The hungry cannot eat promises. It is unlikely that angels will appear on the scene to ease their burdens. Humans helping humans is the way to go. Not the only way to go, say those who believe that miracles are indeed possible. But humans helping humans is a realistic way to go, given the fact that the "miracles" that happen in communities of good and faithful people seem to take a little longer these days.

The Christian citizens' lobby Bread for the World is one way to go. Check it out if you are so inclined. It provides a way for us here in the United States to practice both stewardship and citizenship by calling upon our representatives in government to do what we as a rich and powerful nation can do, namely, help poor countries to help themselves. This means debt relief and large injections of economic development assistance.

Ending hunger is a moral calling. The most important arguments for increasing poverty-focused development assistance are moral. A sense of moral obligation provides the push (the "ought"); and a vision of happy, healthy people ("the common good") provides the pull.

Moral sentiment rises partly from the realization that other people are just like us. When impoverished people get up in the morning they go through the same routines as people in the industrialized world—washing, eating, working, loving, and struggling. At night when they lie down, they too hope for a safe and secure tomorrow. In spite of cultural differences, we are all, ultimately, one human race.

So you might want to look into Bread for the World as a way of following the public policy issues as well as responding to the hunger and famine stories that you encounter in the news. Let those for whom you vote know that you want development assistance and hunger reduction to be locked together in foreign policy. Let them know that you care about the hungry poor here at home. If you want more information, go to www.bread.org.

Consider this kind of involvement your way of being like the boy in today's Gospel story. You can come forward with your "barley loaves and fish," your civic participation, to help share the bread for life with others.

Another dimension of all this, a more directly spiritual, even theological dimension that I would ask you to reflect upon today is the multiplication of Christ's presence in the Eucharist. The Gospel miracle relates to the multiplication of loaves of bread. The miracle in every Mass we celebrate relates to the multiplication of the presence of Jesus under the sacramental signs of bread and wine. It is not that we are multiplying the bread on our altars—we are not multiplying the hosts, the Communion breads. What is multiplied is the sacramental presence of Jesus Christ, body and blood (Corpus Christi!), soul and divinity on altars like ours all around the world.

If Jesus could multiply the loaves, as you just heard he did from the Gospel account of Luke—"Then taking the five loaves and the two fish and looking up to heaven, he said the blessing over them, broke them, and gave them to the disciples to set before the crowd"—if Jesus could have done this many centuries ago, why should there be any doubt that he can multiply his presence today in the altar breads that are offered throughout the world in any given Mass?

We believe that he can and does. And we ask the Lord to deepen this belief within us on Corpus Christi Sunday.

VI
Sundays in Ordinary Time

. . . .

35

Second Sunday of the Year

Cana: "Do Whatever He Tells You"

Isaiah 62:1–5; Psalm 96; 1 Corinthians 12:4–11; John 2:1–12

Let me suggest that you imagine yourselves to be, at this moment, waiters and waitresses. Waiting is a faith-based posture. It is a natural stance for any believer. "Wait for the LORD," Psalm 27 instructs you, "take courage; be stouthearted, wait for the LORD." In any case, think of yourself this morning as a waiter or waitress. And then, slip into the shoes of those waiting on table, the servers, in this familiar Gospel story of the wedding feast at Cana.

You know the story. "There was a wedding at Cana in Galilee, and the mother of Jesus was there. Jesus and his disciples were also invited to the wedding." Nice to think of Jesus and Mary as socializing with friends, isn't it; nice to think of them as partygoers, just like you and your friends. But as you know so well from this familiar story, something went wrong at that party. The supply of wine ran out. Mary—sensitive, thoughtful, gentle, resourceful, diplomatic Mary—moved quickly and quietly and came up with a solution that would protect the parents of the bride from exposure to embarrassment.

She turned to her Son, mentioned the problem, ignored, for all practical purposes, his protest that the time had not yet arrived for anything extraordinary or miraculous from him, and turned to the waiters and waitresses (as you should imagine her turning to you this morning) and said, "Do whatever he tells you."

Notice that she did not say, "He will tell you exactly what to do." She seems to be preparing them for an unusual instruction, a direction that may seem a bit strange, but one, strange as it may sound, they should follow: "Do whatever he tells you."

So they did and the rest, as they say, is history—biblical, theological, spiritual, salvation history. It is the kind of history that continues

127

to unfold today in a faith-filled world where believers like yourselves try your best to be attentive to divine direction and "do whatever he tells you." As you know from personal experience, the direction—the inspiration, the impulse, that gentle push or pull that registers within—can sound a bit strange, can bring with it some initial unease. "Do whatever he tells you."

What might that be at this stage of your life? Think about that today.

The Cana story is rich in symbolism. Mary is a type here, a figure, of the Church. The Church, like Mary, intervenes or intercedes on our behalf through its sacramental ministries, and we, before our time, receive manifestations of divine power. Because the Church asks and acts, we have new wine, new life, new joy. Our watery weakness is turned, by sacramental grace, into spiritual strength.

Water into wine at the Cana wedding feast symbolizes both baptism and the Eucharist. The waters of baptism initiate divine life in the person who is baptized. Through the words of institution spoken by an ordained minister of the Church, ordinary bread and wine are changed into the body and blood of Christ on altars all over the world. You and all your brothers and sisters in the human community are invited to a wedding feast now, a Eucharistic banquet, a *sacrum convivium*, where there is, right now, abundant spiritual food and drink for your soul, nourishment for the life that began with baptism. You and all your brothers and sisters in the human community are invited to an eternal wedding feast, a heavenly banquet that will last forever. Any wedding feast here on earth can serve to remind you of that fact. The wedding feast at Cana certainly suggests that something greater, something far greater than Cana, is in store for those who believe. Just "do whatever he tells you," and you will find your way there.

Cana is another epiphany. There are three epiphanies—the "showing forth," the manifestation of Christ's divinity—in the liturgy. The first we celebrated with the journey of the Magi to the manger; the second we saw in recent Gospel readings of the baptism of Jesus by John at the River Jordan when the heavens opened and the voice of the Father broke through with an expression of divine pleasure in God's divine Son. It was as if a shaft of light came down from the heavens and focused on him. And the third epiphany is the "sign" given here at Cana.

"Jesus did this as the beginning of his signs at Cana in Galilee and so revealed his glory, and his disciples began to believe in him."

So Cana is really an invitation to faith in the divinity of Christ. Let the evidence of Cana help you to be a believer. And, as any believer will tell you, it takes faith to "do whatever he tells you."

As you thank God today for the gift of faith, as you adore Christ again today, be mindful of the demands of faith. Be mindful also of the need for prayer to discern correctly what demands faith might now be putting upon you. No matter what he tells you, be sure to do it. Remaining in your waiter/waitress role, you will agree, I think, that there must have been an air of confidence in Mary's voice and manner when she spoke to those who were waiting on table. And you might also agree that they surely caught something of that confidence when, not knowing exactly what would happen, they went promptly and expectantly to fill the jars with water. So go ahead, whenever the Spirit prompts you, and fill your jars. Who knows what will happen?

Mary's instructions to the waiters and waitresses offer you a lesson about prayer. Commenting on her words, the great French Dominican Scripture scholar M.-J. Lagrange has written: "The prayer most certain to be heard is one submitting itself in advance to whatever Jesus would wish." And, of course, the miracle at Cana demonstrates so beautifully how Jesus justified the absolute trust that Mary placed in him that day.

There are many qualities of Mary that are beyond the reach of our ability to imitate, but faith and trust are not among them. Just trust, and wait. Cana will break into your own personal experience sometime soon.

36

Third Sunday of the Year

Inaugural Address: "The Spirit of the Lord Is upon Me"

Nehemiah 8:2–4a, 5–6, 8–10; Psalm 19; 1 Corinthians 12:12–30;
Luke 1:1–4; 4:14–21

There are two themes from these readings that I would like to highlight for you today. One is the body image from 1 Corinthians—you, each one and all of you—being parts of and constituting the body of Christ; and the second theme is inauguration, particularly the inaugural address given by Jesus in the synagogue at Nazareth as he began his public life.

There is, of course, an inauguration weekend in Washington, DC, every four years. A new or reelected president takes the oath of office, delivers an inaugural address, views a parade, enjoys the inaugural ball, and then settles down to the business of governing a nation that sees itself as "one nation under God," a nation that is "indivisible," a nation that offers to its citizens the promise that they will find here "liberty and justice for all" (although I once heard a prominent member of the Congress while reciting the pledge of allegiance on the House floor, say, *sotto voce*, "liberty and justice for almost everyone").

The president gives us words of inauguration. The newly inaugurated president has to look to the citizens he leads—to elected representatives and to all the rest of us—to put legs under his ideas, to quite literally lend the helping hands needed to put his programs into place. The forty-third President of the United States George W. Bush said, "I will work to build a single nation of justice and opportunity." He announced a "new commitment to live out our nation's promise," and acknowledged that "while many of our citizens prosper, others doubt the promise even the justice of our own country." Mr. Bush said in his inaugural address, "Americans in need are not problems but priorities," and added what sounded like an invitation to all of us to help: "Compassion is the work of a nation, not just a government," he said.

Even though his promise of a tax cut drew the most applause, we hoped that the part of his speech where he asked the nation to "seek a common good beyond your comfort," would not be ignored. What he may have overlooked or left unsaid in his brief inaugural address, but what surely had to be done if the common good was to be served, can only be done by us, by the great body of citizens who empower leadership in this representative democracy, and who, at times, must exercise leadership by prodding their elected leaders to action. "Our public interest depends on private character," the new president said. And he was right. What he said meant that the years of his presidency (any presidency, really) would be a test of character—his and ours—and we have to examine our potential as Christians for measuring up to that test.

When he took the oath of office in 2009, Barack Obama said, among other things, "To the people of poor nations, we pledge to work alongside you to make your farms flourish and let clean waters flow; to nourish starved bodies and feed hungry minds. And to those nations like ours that enjoy relative plenty, we say we can no longer afford indifference to suffering outside our borders; nor can we consume the world's resources without regard to effect. For the world has changed, and we must change with it."

So, on any inaugural weekend, we should reflect on the words and example of Jesus at the beginning of his public life. He "returned to Galilee in the power of the Spirit," Luke's Gospel tells us, "and news of him spread throughout the whole region. He taught in their synagogues and was praised by all." (His first 100 days apparently went quite well!) "He came to Nazareth, where he had grown up, and went according to his custom into the synagogue on the sabbath day. He stood up to read and was handed a scroll of the prophet Isaiah." (You will notice that he had a speech writer of impeccable credentials!) So Jesus unrolled the scroll and began to read these famous words:

The Spirit of the Lord is upon me, because he has anointed me to bring glad tidings to the poor. He has sent me to proclaim liberty to captives and recovery of sight to the blind, to let the oppressed go free, and to proclaim a year acceptable to the Lord.

Jesus drew upon Isaiah to construct both a platform and a program: (1) to bring glad tidings to the poor; (2) to proclaim liberty to captives; (3) and recovery of sight to the blind; (4) to let the oppressed go free, and (5) to proclaim a year acceptable to the Lord ("acceptable" in the sense of something along the lines of the ancient jubilee year of forgiveness and reconciliation, particularly forgiveness of debt).

God made some important promises through his prophets, like Isaiah, to the economically, physically, and socially unfortunate, and Jesus is here to deliver on those promises. In his inaugural address Jesus spoke words of promise and encouragement to the poor, the sick, the systematically oppressed, the imprisoned (particularly those imprisoned with, by, and for indebtedness), and to those who were downtrodden—emotionally, physically, socially, and economically put upon, crushed. What did it mean to them to hear him say, "Today this Scripture passage is fulfilled in your hearing."? It would mean very little to them unless others—those with power and influence—also heard these words and decided to act on them. So, when his inaugural address was finished, Jesus stepped out from that synagogue and walked about that town and eventually that whole region preaching, teaching, setting admirable example, and inviting all—poor and rich, weak and powerful—to follow him, to believe his Gospel and to act upon it by addressing the causes of poverty, chronic illness, and the other forms of oppression that weighed upon the little people, the weak, sick, and powerless.

He did that for three years and attracted a band of disciples. They in turn went out preaching and teaching and spreading the good news. They took their places in the daily doings of ordinary life and from those places did what they could to address the problems Jesus cited in his inaugural address. They did what they could, generation after generation, but much remains to be done today. By whom? By us—by we who call ourselves Christians, followers of Christ, respondents to his call, including his inaugural call to bring good news to the poor, to captives, to the blind, and to the oppressed.

Jesus and his original band of disciples are not around to meet these responsibilities today. All he has on earth now is us! This sobering reality is imaged so powerfully and well in a saying attributed to St. Teresa of Avila: "Christ has no body now on earth but yours, no hands on earth but yours. Yours are the eyes through which he looks out with compassion upon the world. Yours the feet with which he chooses to go about doing good. For as he is the head, so are you the members, and we are all one in Christ Jesus."

So, I ask you, dear friends in Christ, to listen again to the words of today's second reading—Paul to the Corinthians: "Brothers and sisters: As a body is one though it has many parts, and all the parts of the body, though many, are one body, so also Christ....you are Christ's body."

You should take those words quite literally today as you think about putting legs—your legs—under his inaugural address. Christ no longer walks the earth unless feet like yours are there to take him where he would like to go. He has no hands, unless you offer him your own, to reach out and touch people who live now in oppressive conditions. Yours are quite literally the eyes through which he can look out on our world today, so try to see our world as he might see it. Take his perspective on poverty, on family (and on the anniversary of *Roe v. Wade*, look at abortion through his eyes) Take his perspective on illness and disease, incarceration and capital punishment, oppressive working conditions and repressive rule. Take his perspective on addiction and hunger, on disability and discrimination. Christ has no eyes on earth, but your eyes, so go out and take a look from his perspective. He has no hands on earth, but your hands, so give some thought now to what you might in fact be able to do with your hands, hearts, and minds to make things better in our time.

In the setting of this liturgy, we might well ask, as St. John Chrysostom once asked, "What is the use of loading [Christ's] table with cups of gold, if he himself is perishing from hunger?" Because, you see, dear friends, there on the other side of the body metaphor, the "you-are-Christ's-body" teaching of 1 Corinthians, you see there the shattering truth that Christ is present in the bodies of the poor, the hungry, the blind, the oppressed, the imprisoned, the put-upon. In one of his most moving homilies, John Chrysostom has Christ speak to us about the then of Christ's cross and the now of his crucifixion in these compelling words: "I fasted for you then, and I suffer hunger for you now. I was thirsty when I hung on the cross, and I thirst still in the poor; in both ways to draw you to myself and to make you humane for your own salvation."

It is indeed for your own salvation, not just for the welfare of those far less fortunate than you, it is for your own salvation that you put your legs under Christ's program, that you lend your hands to implementing his inaugural policies. The new beginning that comes every fourth year on inauguration weekend opens another chapter in the story, not just the story of what President Bush called America's "flawed and fallible people," but of salvation history as well. Mr. Bush put himself on record with the conviction that "everyone belongs, everyone deserves a chance, no insignificant person was ever born." He reminded the nation that "where there is suffering there is duty." And he made this commitment: "When we see that wounded traveler on the road to Jericho, we will not pass to the other side." Nice words, now embalmed in print, all but lost to memory.

So remember, "Christ has no body now on earth but yours, no hands on earth but yours. Yours are the eyes through which he looks out with compassion upon the world. Yours the feet with which he chooses to go about doing good. For as he is the head, so are you the members, and we are all one in Christ Jesus."

Presidents come and go; and so does inaugural rhetoric. But Jesus Christ is "the same yesterday, today, and forever" (Heb 13:8), and his inaugural address, recorded for you in today's Gospel reading, remains to challenge all who follow him.

There is work now to be done in our nation by Republicans and Democrats alike, by young and old, by privileged and poor, by all citizens together. We, as Catholic Christian citizens of both this earthly city and the City of God, have, in the Scriptures we've been considering today, powerful motivation for doing our part.

37

Fourth Sunday of the Year

"Love Is Patient, Love Is Kind"

Jeremiah 1:4–5, 17–19; Psalm 71; 1 Corinthians 12:31—13:13;
Luke 4:21–30

Today's second reading—from Paul's First Letter to the Corinthians—
is familiar to all of us; it's a favorite at weddings, as you well know.
I've often suggested to newlyweds that if they have a friend who is a
calligrapher, they should ask that person to produce this passage from
1 Corinthians 13 on a page that is suitable for framing. It belongs in
every Christian heart and home; it is both a mission statement and
strategic plan not just for a happy marriage, but also for anyone's success (married or single, young or old, male or female) in achieving the
Christian community's goal of loving one another.

I want to attempt today to put a human face on Paul's detailed outline of the "still more excellent way" that we should follow in striving
"for the greatest spiritual gifts." St. Paul says that love is patient and
kind, never jealous, not pompous, not inflated, never rude, does not
seek its own interests. Love, according to Paul, is not quick-tempered;
it does not brood over injury. It does not rejoice over wrongdoing but
rejoices with the truth. Love "bears all things, believes all things, hopes
all things, endures all things." Love "never fails." St. Paul advises that
when you line up the three great theological virtues (theological in the
sense of having God as their primary object), when you compare faith,
hope, and love, "the greatest of these is love."

But what is the meaning of love? What in the practical order of
things does all this mean?

Popular culture often devalues, even debases the meaning of love.
Pulp fiction doesn't help, although good literature always sheds light
on the deeper truths. MTV is not helpful in pointing the young in the
direction of the true reality of love. Most films and popular televised

stories are shallow in this respect; some are simply fraudulent and cynically deceptive when it comes to touching on the meaning of love.

Northern Virginia novelist Richard Bausch made this interesting point in an interview with the *Washington Post* (March 2, 1992):

> When I go to the movies and they walk off into the happy sunset, I always wonder about three years down the road, with a baby crying and sour stomach…It's like a form of spiritual arthritis [he's referring to his own outlook]—when the person comes down the stairs, I see the inevitable bad outcome. To me love doesn't reside in all those pretty sunsets. Love isn't there, love is the daily stuff, the way we live our lives. What interests me is all those areas—those irredeemable sorrows we have to deal with.

Love is indeed "the daily stuff." But the sorrows associated with love are not, as Richard Bausch suggests, "irredeemable," they are a positive part of the daily "stuff" of life that can tell you a lot about love.

"Love in action is a harsh and dreadful thing compared to love in dreams," is a quotation from *The Brothers Karamozov* that Dorothy Day was fond of repeating. Dreams are not the stuff of solid marriages. Here is how the playwright and humorist James Thurber put the issue in an essay many years ago in an issue of *Life* magazine dedicated to an exploration of the state of marriage and family in the United States:

> My pet antipathy is the bright detergent voice of the average American singer, male or female, yelling or crooning in cheap yammer songs of the day about "love." Americans are brought up without being able to tell love from sex, lust, Snow White, or Ever After. We think of it as a push-button solution, or instant cure, for discontent and a sure road to happiness, whatever it is. By our sentimental ignorance we encourage marriage as a kind of tranquilizing drug. A lady of 47 who has been married 27 years and has six children knows what love really is and once described it for me like this: "Love is what you've been through with somebody."

Now, listen to the wisdom of the Church on this subject; it is captured in an "exhortation" that used to be read by the priest to every bride and groom about to exchange their marriage vows. This was back in the days before the Latin Mass gave way to the vernacular languages. These words were in English—straightforward, powerful, moving English prose. Some of you may recall hearing them on your own wedding day. They are words of wisdom for all of us, married or not, because they encapsulate what it means to lay down your life for another, and that, of course, is the New Commandment of love given to us by Jesus at the Last Supper, a commandment that each of us has to obey if we wish to call ourselves Christian.

"Beloved of Christ," the priest would say to the bride and groom decades ago,

> ...you are about to enter upon a union which is most sacred and most serious....This union...is most serious because it will bind you together for life in a relationship so close and so intimate, that it will profoundly influence your whole future. That future with its hopes and disappointments, its successes and its failures, its pleasures and its pains, its joys and its sorrows, is hidden from your eyes. You know that these elements are mingled in every life and are to be expected in your own....
>
> Because these [vows you are about to pronounce] involve such solemn obligations, it is most fitting that you rest the security of your wedded life upon the great principle of self-sacrifice....Sacrifice is usually difficult and irksome. Only love can make it easy, and perfect love can make it a joy. We are willing to give in proportion as we love. And when love is perfect the sacrifice is complete.

So the Church in its wisdom has been saying over the centuries that the meaning of love is sacrifice, and the meaning of sacrifice is love. "There is nothing," St. Teresa of Avila once remarked, "that cannot be borne with cheerful alacrity by those who love one another."

Many years ago, Boyd Barrett wrote a book called *Life Begins with Love*. Listen to this short paragraph; it puts a very human face on what Paul described as "love" to the Christians of Corinth:

Love is a young soldier at the front, scared and miserable, who writes a cheerful letter home to his parents. Love is a man who promises to find a job for an unfortunate misfit and keeps his promise. Love is a woman, who, on discovering another woman's shameful secret, does not reveal it. Love is a thrifty housewife who takes the best she has in her icebox to lay before an unwanted guest and serves him with style on her best table linen. Love is a college boy who learns the deaf alphabet in order to converse with a lonely old lady who cannot hear. Love is the one who gives abundantly and gives gladly when a beggar returns to ask another alms. Love is the person who, instead of recriminating, sees his own shortcomings in another's faults. Love is the grateful soul who remembers his indebtedness and repays as best he can. (Milwaukee: Bruce Publishing Co., 1952, p. 6.)

As the late Jesuit theologian and noted homilist Fr. Walter Burghardt once put it: "Love is, first of all, sacrifice. Not tragic sacrifice, nor tearful sacrifice. Love is giving without hope of receiving. Love is burying dead who do not answer, and clothing naked who do not thank. Love is unselfishly wishing good to others. It is just the opposite of that all-too-human tendency to be bitterly jealous of joy in another's eyes, of the health in another's body, of honor in another's life and prosperity in another's home." In one of his many books Fr. Burghardt calls upon Christians to drive hatred from their hearts and to begin to live in love: "I am asking you to tear hate and envy out of your hearts, to give something of yourself to every human being who enters your little world, to pray God's blessing on the Judas who has betrayed you and the Herod who has laughed at you and the Pilate who has washed his hands of you. God does not ask you to like them, but he does insist that you love them. Love them not with the surface love that means moonlight and roses, but with the true love that wills what God knows as best for them, that prays for what is for their genuine happiness, that does something concrete to realize it... Be afraid not to love those whom Christ himself loves because they are sons [and daughters] of the same Father. In short, love one another as he has loved you."

What then is love? Cheerful sacrifice. "There is nothing that cannot be borne with cheerful alacrity by those who love one another." Be kind, be considerate, be Christian. That's the point Paul was making to the Corinthians when he explained that love is patient and kind, never jealous, not pompous, not inflated, never rude, does not seek its own interests. Love is not quick-tempered; it does not brood over injury. It does not rejoice over wrongdoing but rejoices with the truth. Love "bears all things, believes all things, hopes all things, endures all things." Love "never fails."

This is not news to anyone of you, but it is "good news" to the world, the good news that you as followers of Christ are expected to share. As the old song put it so well, "What the world need now is love sweet love, that's the only thing that there's just too little of...."

Now that you've refreshed your memory on the meaning of true love, go out once again—go home, go to work, go out into the community—and give it a try!

38

Fifth Sunday of the Year

Vocations: "'Here I am,' I said, 'send me!'"

Isaiah 6:1–2a, 3–8; Psalm 138; 1 Corinthians 15:1–11; Luke 5:1–11

You heard the voice of the prophet Isaiah in today's first reading. You heard him expressing his unworthiness before God: "Woe is me, I am doomed! I am a man of unclean lips…yet my eyes have seen the… Lord of Hosts!" And you heard Isaiah recount how one of the seraphim flew down from above the throne of God holding an ember taken with tongs from a fire at God's high altar. And the angel touched Isaiah's mouth with the burning ember saying, "See, now that this has touched your lips, your wickedness is removed, your sin purged." And Isaiah says, "Then I heard the voice of the Lord saying, 'Whom shall I send? Who will go for us?'" "Here I am," Isaiah said, "send me!"

"Here I am, Lord, send me." Let that be your prayer today: "Here I am, Lord, send me!" Send you where? For what? And when will God send you? Set those questions aside for a moment.

In Isaiah's story, Yahweh is depicted as a king in need of messengers, a leader in need of help.

In the Gospel story you heard this morning from St. Luke, the God-man Jesus is pictured in a natural and familiar setting—alongside a lake, mixing with fishermen who were repairing their nets. He steps into one of their boats, one that belongs to Simon, and pushes off a bit from shore. And from the boat, he taught the crowds gathered along the shoreline. When he finished teaching, he apparently decided to display his supernatural power, to establish, if you will, his credentials with these good but ordinary fishermen—men who, much like Isaiah, tended to focus on their unworthiness. Jesus instructs them to move out into deeper waters; he sets them up for a miraculous catch of fish, a great haul, so great that their nets snapped under the weight. "When

Simon Peter saw this, he fell at the knees of Jesus and said, 'Depart from me, Lord, for I am a sinful man.'" (Echoes of Isaiah!—"Woe is me, I am doomed! For I am a man of unclean lips.") Look again at Peter: "For astonishment at the catch of fish they had made seized him and all those with him....Jesus said to Simon, 'Do not be afraid; from now on you will be catching men.'"

"Fishers of men," as the expression came down to us through the centuries; "fishers of men and women," as we would want to say today. Does any of that apply to any of you?

Like the king in the Isaiahan story who said, "Whom shall I send? Who will go for us?" Jesus by the lakeside is saying, in effect, I need help. I need helpers like these fellows to help me in this enterprise I'm launching now for the salvation of souls. I'll try to attract good men like these, and women too, who, like Isaiah, may not think they are any great shakes but I know their potential. So I'll ask them for help and hope they say, "Here I am, Lord, send me!"

Some whom Jesus calls will be like Paul who persecuted Jesus—Paul who referred to himself, as you heard him in today's second reading, as "the least of the apostles, not fit to be called an apostle, because I persecuted the church of God." "But," St. Paul goes on to say, "by the grace of God I am what I am, and his grace to me has not been ineffective." How about his grace to you?

So, you're not perfect, but so what? You can still say, "Here I am, Lord, send me."

I must tell you today, dear friends, something that you already know, namely, that there is a need for priests in the Roman Catholic Church. Can any of you here today say, "Here I am, Lord, send me" to meet that need?

All of you who are female will say with varying measures of feeling, "No, I can't meet that need because they won't let me!" Some of you women might be inclined to add: "If the Church would lighten up, and open up the priesthood to me, I might give it some thought." But that opening up is not likely to happen any day soon, as we all know, and we still have to deal with the problem of a priest shortage now, right here in the United States.

Even so, some of you might say, "Well, it is really not such a big a problem after all. Look at the great numbers of competent, generous, and impressive lay men and women who are clearly responding to a call to ministry in the Church today, doing much of the work that priests used to do." Good point. But when to that excellent point the additional observation is made that the priest shortage is not real, I cannot agree. We still need priests. The men and women who, since Vatican II, have become servant leaders in our Church clearly have vocations to ministry, but do they (or should they) have vocations to ordained ministry? And if they don't, are there others out there who might be called to priesthood?

Sociologists have surveyed young college-age Catholics regarding their attitudes toward careers in ministry in the Church. They find an enormous reservoir of generosity and genuine interest in ministry, but not ordained ministry. When researchers probe the reasons why, they identify several institutional barriers: (1) celibacy (the sexual revolution has had its impact on vocations to priesthood), (2) the requirement for priests of a permanent lifelong commitment (if there were something like the military model with a twenty-year enlistment, some young people say that priesthood would be a more attractive option to them), and (3) the exclusion of women from holy orders (which some men take as a proxy for institutional injustice in the Church). Researchers also identify a cultural characteristic that helps to explain the present priest shortage—a tendency on the part of the young to remain uncommitted, or, to put it another way, a cultural hesitation to make permanent commitments (and, as you know, only the really committed need apply for ordination to the priesthood!).

Only those ready to commit themselves can say, "Here I am, Lord, send me!"

Let me hasten to add that the problem is by no means restricted to the young and restless, to those of eligible age to be candidates for holy orders. Parents today are not storming heaven with prayers that their offspring will be called to priesthood or religious life. That fact is worth examining because without parental encouragement, the young are far less likely to consider priesthood and religious life.

Among the personal effects left behind by Fr. John W. Tynan, SJ, after his death in 1960, was a letter from his father, received shortly after young Jack Tynan left his home in Jersey City to enter the Jesuit novitiate in 1919. His dad, expressing a deep and beautiful faith, wrote to his son in these words:

> You gave me one of the greatest joys of my life when you told me you had joined the Jesuits. I never mentioned a vocation to you because I believe the Almighty reserves calling men to the priesthood to Himself. Years before the Holy Hour was begun in St. Bridget's, I used to have one on my own on Saturday nights. I never could meditate, so I prayed and hoped and begged and cried, yes, and sometimes I fell asleep, all in one hour. You were often the subject of my thoughts. I said many a time to our blessed Lord, "I'll waive the pleasure of ever seeing his back at the altar as a priest, only call him—for Kalamazoo, or Hong Kong, or Jersey City."

Shortly after writing that letter, Mr. Tynan died. With him went an era characterized not only by the "Holy Hour" and the priest not facing the congregation when he celebrated Mass, but also by tears and prayers focused on the call to priesthood for one's son. It would be rare today, not impossible, but surely rare, to hear a father describe his reaction to a son's decision to enter the seminary as "one of the greatest joys of my life."

Why don't fathers pray today as Jack Tynan's father did? Where is the Church that fostered such prayer? Fathers still pray, of course, and the institutional Church is still very much present in our midst, but the sociological surroundings are markedly different. They are splitting at several prominent seams: (1) many decades of seeing men leave the priesthood (thus raising the question, "Why?"); (2) public evidence of scandal and misconduct in the priesthood (prompting the "steer clear of that crowd" reaction); (3) debate about the desirability of having a married Roman Catholic clergy (suggesting the question, "Why not?"); and (4) plenty of talk about the possibility of women priests in the Catholic Church (keeping alive the question of whether this is something that would be clearly impossible for an all-powerful God to bring about).

A man who entered the seminary before and during the Second Vatican Council (1962–1965) came out of a world that no longer exists and offered himself for service in a Church that now no longer exists. In the old days, priesthood was a "step up" socially in the Catholic community; that's no longer the case. The old Catholic culture saw priests as "necessary" for "saving souls" and Catholic schools were seen as "fortresses of the faith" that simply had to be staffed. So all the "faithful" paid up generously—the laity with their money and with the "gift" of sons or daughters; priests and religious paid with their lives. Their motivation for the generosity and the sacrifice associated with entering a seminary or novitiate was in some measure related to "saving my own soul and the souls of others," and that motivation was sometimes tinged with fear. Today there is less anxiety about saving "my" soul or the souls of others, not because the actual barriers to entry to eternal life have been lowered, and not through any disinterest in salvation, but for other good reasons that indicate a more healthy adjustment to the world. Presumption may be on the rise, but whatever the cause, there is a lot less fear these days of losing one's soul by refusing the call. So why let avoidance of hell or "saving" the souls of others dominate one's vocational decision making? Saving souls—working with and for God in God's work of saving souls—is still and always will be an important concern.

We need good men in the priesthood today. We certainly want many more good men in the Jesuit order, the Society of Jesus. I stand before you today to ask good men—not perfect men, but good men like Isaiah, Paul, and Peter—to consider a vocation to priesthood. Consider other vocations as well, of course, including vocations to non-ordained ministry in the Church. But don't neglect to include the possibility of priesthood. And I ask all of you to join me in praying that more young men will answer that call.

Priests are "fishers" in the service of Christ, fishers of men and women in need of salvation. Ministry—ordained ministry—is still, in God's mysterious providence, necessary for salvation. There is still a harvest to be brought in by priestly ministry. We don't need men who are afraid of the world, or afraid of losing their souls if they reject a call to priesthood. We don't need men who are afraid of their sexuality and who might see celibacy as a pre-packaged remedy for that fear. We don't need men who don't feel up to the demands of scientific careers, or the competition of business, or the demands of other professions. We need generous men with a high-hearted love of Christ who want to serve God's people by proclaiming God's word, ministering the sacraments of salvation, and, along with lay associates, staffing and administering and delivering the social, educational, and health services the Church provides.

And we need all of you—men and women, young and old—to pray to the Lord of the harvest to call talented and generous men to priesthood along with the many talented and generous men and women he is calling to non-ordained ministries in this great Church that we all call home. Individuals have to examine their hearts to see where, when, and to what God might be calling them. And both leadership and followership in the Church have to face up to the demands of both courage and wisdom in examining the barriers—the institutional barriers to entry—that are discouraging decisions on the part of the generous young to choose to commit themselves to priesthood.

All of us have to reflect on and pray about this issue. In one way or another each one of us has to say within our hearts today, "Here I am, Lord, send me!"—send me, like Jack Tynan, to priesthood, or like Jack Tynan's dad, to prayer for priestly vocations, or like Isaiah, Paul, Peter, Andrew and the other apostles, to proclaim the good news, or like so many faithful folk you meet in daily life, to be by your example, good news of salvation to a world in need of help.

39

Sixth Sunday of the Year

"Blessed Are You"

Jeremiah 17:5–8; Psalm 1; 1 Corinthians 15:12, 16–20;
Luke 6:17, 20–26

It is nice, isn't it, when you sneeze, to hear someone say, "God bless you!" Well, although there were no sneezes in the congregation today before the Gospel was read, the words from Luke's Gospel, that you just heard proclaimed, are the words of Jesus saying "Blessed are you." Blessed are you poor, blessed are you who are hungry, blessed are you who are weeping....Blessed are you!

You recognize these as the "beatitudes," the blessings, the happiness sayings that are central to the good news proclaimed by Jesus when he walked the earth. Let them come alive again for you today. Hear Jesus proclaiming the beatitudes. Hear him saying, in effect, God has blessed you.

Notice that the version you heard today from the Gospel of Luke says "blessed are you who are poor," not, as Matthew's Gospel puts it, "blessed are the poor in spirit." Reflection on Matthew's version typically leads us to conclude that we should be detached from material things, that we should not permit ourselves to be possessed by our possessions. We can still have money and possessions, perhaps even become rich, we should just not permit ourselves to be prisoners of our possessions. Thus free, we will be happy—men and women of the beatitudes, as Matthew presents them. Here we are. We still show up on Sunday to give thanks!

It is a slightly different story when you listen to the version you have in today's Gospel reading of the beatitudes according to St. Luke. Luke is straightforward, demanding, tough. He has Jesus put it to you directly: "Blessed are you who are poor," not poor in spirit, but the genuinely poor. They're the special ones, the favored ones, they are the really blest.

That makes all of us who live on the positive side of the poverty line a bit uneasy and uncomfortable, to say the least. If I'm not poor—really poor—am I not blest? Is this what this Gospel is saying? Am I not worthy of God's special care and love if I happen to possess a nice share of this world's goods? Don't we consider ourselves blessed by God if we enjoy a good job, a good home, and a nice level of comfort and security? Yes, we do and we should, but Luke's rather stark presentation of the beatitudes should serve to remind that there are genuinely poor people in our midst and that they are not only not forgotten by God, they are favorites in God's eye. God loves them and cares for them and is expecting us—those who are better off, those who are in positions of power and influence—to have special regard for the poor. Our Church, in its great tradition of Catholic social teaching, calls for a preferential option—or preferential love for the poor.

This is not to say that God has no interest in or love for those who are well off. It is not to say that those who have material wealth are not the constant objects of God's unfailing love. It is simply to say that God's love for the poor is special, but not exclusive, and those of us who are not poor are also loved by a God who expects us to join him in his preferential love for the poor and vulnerable.

If you are well off but not grateful enough to remember and share with the poor, you are really not grateful enough! You cannot claim to be grateful for your blessings if you don't share your blessings with the poor, if you don't use your position of power and influence to help the poor.

Poverty is sustained deprivation. The poor are deprived of income, employment, education, food, housing, healthcare, and other necessities of life. You have to ask to what extent what you do, or fail to do, is helping to sustain that deprivation. Why do the poor seem always to be with us? That is a question that looks to the sustaining social structures that keep poverty in place; that is a question that looks to the negligent indifference of those who have, relative to the needs of those who have not.

And serious reflection on the beatitudes demands of us a level of honesty that refuses to put the blame on the poor for their own poverty. Can anyone seriously blame poor infants and children for their poverty? Can anyone blame those unjustly deprived of education and economic opportunity for the poverty that comes to them as a consequence of those deprivations? The casualties are out there. The human need is pressing and real. The Gospel invites us all to open our eyes and see the need, and then we should open our minds to search for long-term solutions as we open our hearts (and wallets) to offer direct help.

Today's Gospel puts a bit of a wake-up call, a gentle prodding—you might even call it a threat—in front of you. Listen again to the "woes" that Luke delivers for your attention: "But woe to you who are rich, for you have received your consolation. But woe to you who are filled now, for you will be hungry. Woe to you who laugh now, for you will grieve and weep."

Step outside yourself and look around. You've often heard the exhortation that you should "wake up and smell the coffee." Well, Luke's Gospel is saying to you today that you should be mindful of your great blessings and let your gratitude for them prompt you to do something to bring those blessings to the less fortunate.

You can do something personally and professionally—you know what you can do, I don't. You can do something through political participation, through volunteer activity, through entrepreneurial initiatives, through charitable contributions—you know what you might do, I don't. Those of you who are young should be thinking of vocational choices that relate to these challenges. Will what you do with your life make any difference at all relative to the problems of poverty, hunger, and injustice in the world? You know what you might do with your life, I don't.

All I can say to all of you is: Don't permit yourself to become distracted from the real problems in your world. Don't let the pursuit of pleasure derail you from the tough work of preparing yourself intellectually and spiritually to make the pursuit of happiness—beatitude kind of happiness—a visible reality in your world today.

40

Seventh Sunday of the Year

"Forgive and You Will Be Forgiven"

1 Samuel 26:2, 7–9, 12–13, 22–23; Psalm 103;
1 Corinthians 15:45–49; Luke 6:27–38

Just imagine what the world would be like tomorrow if all the Christians who heard this Gospel that is being proclaimed today in every corner of the world, were to listen intently, heed the message, and put it into practice. Hear once again the words Luke has Jesus saying to his disciples (a message that Jesus would surely repeat to you today): "Stop judging and you will not be judged. Stop condemning and you will not be condemned. Forgive and you will be forgiven. Give, and gifts will be given to you; a good measure, packed together, shaken down, and overflowing, will be poured into your lap. For the measure with which you measure will in return be measured out to you."

There you have the makings of a personal transformation and a social revolution! Just imagine what the world would be like on Monday morning if all the Sunday churchgoers throughout the world who heard those words translated them into action!

Not one of you rules the world, of course, but you do have some jurisdiction over yourself and your own little corner of the world. Will anything be different there tomorrow because of what you heard and took to heart today? "Stop judging and you will not be judged. Stop condemning and you will not be condemned. Forgive and you will be forgiven. Give, and gifts will be given to you; a good measure, packed together, shaken down, and overflowing, will be poured into your lap. For the measure with which you measure will in return be measured out to you."

I can't stop judging, you might say; the mind was made to judge and mine is always at work. True enough. But must all of your judgments be negative? Need any of them be harsh? Even when your judgment

149

is correctly and appropriately negative, must you always act negatively, must you always be ready to condemn? Of course not. You can be cheerfully and charitably firm; you can be creatively positive even when the judgment is negative. Sometimes that judgment is best kept to yourself; it doesn't have to be announced for the whole world to hear!

Be careful if you find yourself taking a bit, or more than a bit, of delight in the disclosure of weaknesses or misfortunes of others. You have your own weaknesses and vulnerabilities to be concerned about. Think about that, "for the measure with which you measure will in return be measured out to you."

Now that is not the most noble of motives—that is, deciding not to go negative only because you want to fend off negatives that might otherwise come to you. Nothing wrong in letting that less-than-perfect motive go to work for you. Whatever your motive, be positive and be amazed at all the positive things that will come your way. You can count on that happening. You have it on the word of Jesus Christ.

Jesus said to his disciples: "But to you who hear I say, love your enemies, do good to those who hate you, bless those who curse you, pray for those who mistreat you. To the person who strikes you on one cheek, offer the other one as well, and from the person who takes your cloak, do not withhold even your tunic. Give to everyone who asks of you, and from the one who takes what is yours do not demand it back. Do to others as you would have them do to you." This is Jesus speaking, not some loony lightweight social reformer. This is Jesus Christ, true God, true man, speaking to you person-to-person, heart-to-heart, assuming, of course, that your person and heart are ready to respond. As I said, what a revolution there would be—what an attitudinal turnaround there would be in our world tomorrow, if the words of Christ proclaimed from countless pulpits today were heard and heeded throughout the Christian world.

"Forgive and you will be forgiven," Jesus says. Did you ever say, or hear someone else say, "I can never forgive him, I can never forgive her?" Or worse, "I will never forgive; I simply will not do it!" If you've been hurt, treated badly, even unjustly, you will, of course, find it hard to forgive. If you have been treated really badly, you're not caught up in the petty spiteful stuff; you are suffering a deep and painful hurt. Sure, it hurts. Of course, you've been wronged. Undoubtedly it is difficult to forgive, but forgive you must.

The healing power of forgiveness—healing for you and your hurts—cannot be overemphasized. Whether given or received, forgiveness heals. Think of how God has forgiven you. Think now of how you have to forgive those who hurt you.

In a book called *Hearts That We Broke Long Ago* (Bantam, 1983), the Canadian writer Merle Shain wrote: "Until one forgives, life is governed by an endless cycle of resentments and retaliations, and we spend our days scratching at the scabs of the wounds that we sustained long ago instead of letting them dry up and disappear. There is no way to hate another that does not cost the hater, no way to remain unforgiving without maiming yourself, because undissolved anger stutters through the body of the person who cannot forgive."

That "undissolved anger" can be a source of depression; it can help explain why you might not be feeling as well as you could be feeling if only you would let yourself forgive. You could be "maiming yourself" because of your refusal to forgive another.

Listen carefully today to yourself as you say with all the others in this worshipping community the Lord's Prayer. You recite that prayer often; it is part of every Mass. "Forgive us our trespasses, as we forgive those who trespass against us." Realize that in making this prayer, you are asking to be forgiven on a contingent basis. You are declaring yourself willing to be forgiven only if you forgive others. This is a remarkable standard. No one is perfect, of course, but no one can dodge that standard. The stakes are high. The choice is yours.

"Forgive and you will be forgiven." Refuse to forgive.... Well I'll leave it to you to complete that sentence.

We have a lot to ponder in this morning's Gospel reading. Let the pondering begin. You'll be a better person for it. And as your pondering leads to action, you will be making a remarkable contribution toward building a better world.

41

Eighth Sunday of the Year

"Each Tree Is Known by Its Yield"

Sirach 27:4–7; Psalm 92; 1 Corinthians 15:54–58; Luke 6:39–45

In television or radio news interviews, an announcer usually provides an introductory comment, a contextual statement, that is known in the trade as a "setup" piece. In today's collection of Scripture readings, an excerpt from the Book of Sirach is used as a "setup" for the somewhat rambling series of lessons that Jesus offers to his disciples (and, of course, to you) in the selection you just heard from the Gospel of Luke. Listen again to the reading from Sirach: "When a sieve [a strainer, a net with many small holes] is shaken, the husks appear; so do people's faults when they speak." The test of a person, according to Sirach, is in his conversation.

The suggestion here is that you should listen to what someone says, run what you hear through a sieve, a mental filter or strainer, and then examine the debris that you have collected in the net—"the husks," as Sirach describes them—to take the measure of, or evaluate the quality of the person speaking.

By examining his or her external expression, you can determine the internal character of the speaker. Your evaluation will turn up all sorts of "husks"—inanities as well as profanities, non-sequiturs as well as rash judgments, nonsense as well as falsehoods. What you will not have caught in your sieve of examination is the truth and wisdom that have issued forth from the person of integrity; they are not lost; they simply pass through the filter because they are free of husks and impurities. Don't miss the obvious lesson that is there for all of us—watch what you say; unclean speech will betray an unclean heart; falsehoods and outbursts of fury point to deceit and turmoil within the heart of the one who speaks.

"The fruit of a tree shows the care it has had," says Sirach, "so speech discloses the bent of a person's heart."

Turn now to the Gospel reading from Luke who reminds you that Jesus used images in speaking to his disciples. Lots of images here today: the blind leading the blind only to fall in the ditch; students achieving par with their teachers; the "splinter" in your brother's eye compared with the "wooden beam" in your own (I've always found it difficult to imagine how anyone could ignore a plank in his or her own eye, but you get the point). And then Jesus gets to the lesson he wants his disciples to grasp, namely, that "A good tree does not bear rotten fruit, nor does a rotten tree bear good fruit. For every tree is known by its own fruit."

You have to look within. You have to attend to the inside of your house. If there is disorder and disarray within, there will be disorder and disarray outside, all around you.

You will all remember your mother saying to you at one time or another as you were growing up that "one bad apple can spoil the barrel." Bad apples have a way of spreading decay. So avoid the bad apples in your neighborhood; have the right kind of friends.

Not many mothers made the important counterpoint that one good apple can save the whole barrel. (Jesus showed how that can happen.) Concentrate on being a good apple and you'll find yourself making a positive contribution to the supply of goodness in the world. Your integrity can catch on. Your honesty can encourage and enhance the honesty of others. Here's how Jesus made that point in today's Gospel: "A good person out of the store of goodness in his heart produces good, but an evil person out of a store of evil produces evil; for from the fullness of the heart the mouth speaks."

Hard to say how many truly evil persons will hear that Gospel proclaimed today, let alone permit it to turn their lives around. We can pray that this will happen. But we should also turn to ourselves—not looking at anyone else, just at ourselves (forgetting about the "splinter" in another's eye and paying attention to the "wooden beam" in your own, but not letting the presence of that beam discourage you)—and get serious for a moment about your success or failure in permitting what is good within you—and there is so much good within each one of you—to come forth, to be seen, to contribute to the making of a better world.

"Every tree is known by its own fruit," says today's Gospel. Well, you might not like being called a tree—although there's nothing negative intended in that comparison—but take a moment now to examine how you are doing as a tree. What about your yield? How's your foliage? How's your fruit? Should there be a bit more pruning and tilling to make your yield more positive? Are your branches strong? Do you have potential for more growth? Are you getting the proper nutrients?

Jesus had a way of using ordinary—often agricultural—examples to get his points across. Trees are familiar to you all. So think of yourself as a tree for a few moments today. Be grateful that you have a place in the Lord's orchard. Be grateful for the good example the trees around you provide. And be hopeful that this kind of quiet reflection will enhance your value in the forest of faith in which you have been planted.

42

Ninth Sunday of the Year

"I Am Not Worthy to Have You Enter My House"

1 Kings 8:41–43; Psalm 117; Galatians 1:1–2, 6–10; Luke 7:1–10

You meet a centurion in today's Gospel story. A centurion is an officer in the Roman army who has authority over about 100 men; he's a military officer with some experience and no small amount of authority. In this case, this centurion had a personal servant whom he held in high regard and the servant was seriously ill—on the point of death. The centurion knew Jesus by reputation—he had apparently heard of his power to cure and work miracles. So when he learned that Jesus was nearby, he sent several Jewish "elders" out to petition Jesus to come and save the life of the sick servant.

When they address Jesus, the elders speak well of the centurion. They tell Jesus that he is a good man who loves the people under his command. They tell Jesus that he even built a synagogue for the people, and because he is such a good person he "deserves" to be helped, they say. Jesus is responsive to their request so, as the Gospel says, "Jesus went with them." And when Jesus was only a short distance from the centurion's house, the centurion sent out another group of friends to greet Jesus and, speaking for the centurion, they say: "Lord, do not trouble yourself, for I am not worthy to have you enter under my roof." That's a famous phrase that has come down to us in Catholic circles through the liturgy. For centuries we've been saying, just before the reception of Holy Communion, "Lord, I am not worthy that you should enter under my roof, but only say the word and my soul shall be healed" (*et sanabitur anima mea*).

None of us is worthy. That appears to be relatively unimportant to Jesus, the question of worthiness, or deservedness. Despite all the good things the elders said about him, the centurion declared himself to be unworthy. He declared his need, not his merits.

155

Just "say the word," just give the order, says the centurion, through his messengers, to Jesus, and "let my servant be healed." Then, apparently entering into the conversation directly himself, the centurion went on to say to Jesus that he too knows the meaning of an order. He's been giving lots of them as a professional military officer having soldiers under his command. "And I say to one, 'Go,' and he goes; and to another, 'Come here,' and he comes; and to my slave, 'Do this,' and he does it."

Some religious superiors I know—usually rectors of Jesuit communities—often draw on this Scripture passage to joke, in speaking of their men, by remarking, "I say come and they go; I say go and they come!" But there was no joking here on the part of Jesus. He was impressed. The Gospel says that Jesus was amazed "and, turning, said to the crowd following him, 'I tell you, not even in Israel have I found such faith.'" You know how the story ends: "When the messengers returned to the house, they found the slave in good health." That's impressive. Restored to health. Let yourself have a conversation in prayer for a moment now with that servant. What might he have to say to you?

Now you may have noticed that Scripture uses the word "slave" in reference to the servant. Those words are often used interchangeably in Scripture. It is not clear here whether this is an actual case of slavery—ownership of one human being by another, or a servant relationship, not servitude, just service. I mention this just to point out that apparently Jesus did not think it was the time to discuss, let alone condemn, slavery as a social institution. Society had then, as it does now, many ills. You take them on one at a time, when the time is right. Jesus took a pass on slavery here and simply went on to exercise divine power in response to a display of human faith.

That is the message for us today. God does respond to human need when human need is put before him in the vocabulary of faith. You don't have to be perfect to get the attention of the Lord. You don't have to be deserving. You do not draw down God's favor (grace) because you merit it. It helps to acknowledge your unworthiness ("Lord, I am not worthy"), and it is in the context of your unworthiness that Jesus responds. It was not because the centurion built a synagogue for the people, or because he was nice to those under his command—that all helped, I'm sure—but it was his faith that drew the favor of the Lord.

Faith is not bargaining—if you do this, I'll do that. No, faith is entrusting yourself to God, putting your needs, your security, your future in God's hands. Faith is letting go, loving unconditionally. Apparently, Jesus did not see a whole lot of faith when he was traveling around Capernaum in his day. You might fairly ask how much faith he would find if he were walking our streets today.

Faith, of course, is a gift. You don't merit it. You cannot build it up on your own. Think of faith as a bed of embers that has been given to you; it is there within you. What you can do is fan those embers with prayer, with faith-based petitions, and the next thing you know those embers produce flames, you can almost feel the stirrings of faith within you. Those stirrings are not unnoticed by God. They catch God's attention and draw down upon you God's favor.

You may have a "servant" in need of healing. You may have a marriage in need of repair. You may have a spouse in need of work, a child in need of health, a friend in need of confidence. There are many needs that you know to be genuine and by simply naming them, the Lord whom you do not presume to invite into your home, may indeed be so pleased with your expression of faith that the needs you present may indeed be met.

All you can be at moments like this is grateful. All you are expected to be at all times is faithful.

43

Tenth Sunday of the Year

The Widow of Nain

1 Kings 17:17–26; Psalm 30; Galatians 1:11–19; Luke 7:11–17

This is one of my favorite Gospel stories—the account of Jesus bringing back to life the dead son of a widow who lived in a small village called Nain. I like this story for several reasons—it is another demonstration of the power of Jesus; it is a reminder that the divine pity is at work in our world, and it is a good example of how you can look though an event in the public life of Jesus and see hovering over it, if you will, divine power just waiting to break through to meet the need of a simple, unsophisticated person who is hurting. Let me explain that third point first.

You will recall reading in the Gospel of John (14:6–10) that Philip turned one day to Jesus and said, "Master, show us the Father." In response, Jesus said to him: "Have I been with you for so long a time and you still do not know me, Philip? Whoever has seen me has seen the Father." Carry that idea of "whoever sees me sees the Father" with you as you follow Jesus from event to event in the pages of the Gospel. Think of the Gospel as providing you with a "stage" for each event in the public life of Jesus. Imagine that there is a proscenium framing that stage, and let your mind's eye move through the proscenium to rise up to see the divine reality above, namely, the presence of the Father. "Whoever sees me, sees the Father." As you watch Jesus looking with pity, reaching out to help, touching someone in need, as you see the various events, you are seeing behind them and above them, so to speak, the Father's presence, compassion, and power at work in our world.

In this case, you can easily picture the dead man being carried out through the gate of this small town Nain. You can see the stretcher or litter on which the body lies. The Gospel tells you that it is the only son

158

of a widowed mother on that stretcher and that the Lord "was moved with pity for her and said to her, 'Do not weep.'" Then "he stepped forward and touched the coffin; at this the bearers halted."

Remember now, "Whoever sees me sees the Father." What are you seeing here? You are seeing that "strong right arm" of God that the psalmist and the prophets so often speak of; you are seeing it at work. You are seeing the hand of God that "upholds" you, according to the promises you find in Scripture; you are seeing that hand at work. You see this small funeral procession come to a halt and you hear Jesus say, "Young man, I tell you arise!" And there before your eyes: "The dead man sat up and began to speak, and Jesus gave him to his mother." Amazing. You are witnessing an extraordinary event. And because you can separate the event from the mystery that lies behind it and above it, you are observing the power of the eternal Father at work in your own everyday world. Amazing.

That power is still here. That power is still available to meet our needs. And so is the divine pity still with us. It is simply wrong to let yourself imagine your God to be a severe, punishing, judgmental force waiting to pounce upon you. You have to believe, and act as if you believe, that God's pity hovers over you and your world and that God's pity is a powerful force that can overcome death and restore life.

There is no record here of any prayers or petitions made by the widow. The record shows only her tears. And those tears caused Jesus to be moved with pity, and that pity moved the powers of heaven to respond to human need.

It is impossible to measure the enormous reservoir of divine pity that hovers above us. You can't measure it but you can believe it is there. It is quite possible to ignore or forget the fact that there is a reality called divine pity, that it was displayed by Jesus when he walked this earth and acted upon by his Father and the Holy Spirit to ease human suffering. Forgetting that divine pity is there—ready and willing to respond to our needs—we become overwhelmed by the spectacle of sin, suffering, pain and poverty in our world, not to mention the hatred and violence we humans inflict upon one another. We become overwhelmed and immobilized. We fall into indifference and despair.

That is surely not the way God wants us to be. We ignore the divine pity and tax the divine patience—all to our loss and confusion—when we should be exercising our faith, appealing to the divine pity, and invoking divine power to save us from our sin and foolish forgetfulness.

So think today and in some quiet moments of the week to come, think of the power of pity. At one level, you can think of the power of pity in human events—human beings being nice to human beings, but I would hope that you give some thought to the power of pity on a grander scale. Think of the abiding presence of divine pity as a canopy over your world. Think of the reality of divine pity as part of the air you breathe. Think of the power of pity—the enormous reservoir of divine power—waiting to be released in response to the tears and prayers of needy human beings like you and me who should pray far more than we do for the rescue of our world from the forces of evil. The forces of good are greater, we know, than the forces of evil. What we seem not to realize, however, is that the power of pity will show itself in response to our prayers. Wait no longer. Just ask and believe.

44

Eleventh Sunday of the Year

"Your Faith Has Been Your Salvation"

2 Samuel 12:7–10, 13; Psalm 32; Galatians 2:16, 19–21;
Luke 7:36—8:3

The Gospel story today is all about forgiveness. Linkages are also there
to faith and love. Speaking of the sinful woman who receives forgiveness in this story, Jesus says that she was forgiven because "she has
shown great love." And speaking directly to her he says, "Your faith
has saved you; go in peace."

Faith, love, forgiveness. There is not only room, but need, for all
three in each of our lives. Faith comes to you as a gift. Love is your
personal responsibility. Forgiveness is your route to salvation. Each
of these three—faith, love, and forgiveness—deserves more consideration on your part than you are probably inclined to give.

You may take your faith for granted instead of recognizing it an
unmerited gift and thus remaining constantly and consciously grateful.
You may not even give much thought to what faith means, to the reality of faith in any life.

You hear a lot about love and hope you will receive it. But you are
probably somewhat reluctant and perhaps inconsistent in offering your
love to others. And you may not reflect sufficiently on the fact that that
love requires sacrifice, that without sacrifice, there can be no love.

And as for the third notion under consideration—forgiveness—you
may acknowledge that this is not necessarily your strong suit, you may
be aware of a reluctance if not an absolute refusal to forgive.

It often helps, as is the case today, to use the Old Testament read-
ing as a context that will provide a better understanding of the New
Testament reading. In today's first reading, the selection from the
Second Book of Samuel, you see a reference to the egregious sin of
David to whom Nathan speaks. After listing the many favors King

David received, Nathan, speaking for and in the name of the Lord God of Israel, says to David: "Why have you despised the LORD and done evil in his sight? You have cut down Uriah the Hittite with the sword; his wife you took as your own, and him you killed with the sword of the Ammonites." You remember the famous story of David and Bathsheba to which Nathan is referring. And the Scripture account continues: "Then David said to Nathan, 'I have sinned against the LORD.' Nathan answered David: 'The LORD has removed your sin. You shall not die.'"

Immediately, the responsorial psalm (Ps 32) has all of us say, "Lord, forgive the wrong I have done" and that psalm, replete with words of forgiveness, connected you to the second reading, the words you heard from Paul's Letter to the Galatians: Knowing "that a person is not justified by works of the law but through faith in Jesus Christ, even we have believed in Christ Jesus that we may be justified by faith in Christ and not by works of the law." There again you have the notion of faith. Paul proclaims a justification by faith—not by faith alone—but it is faith, not rigid adherence to the law that saves. Christ is living in me, says Paul, "I live by faith in the Son of God, who has loved me and given himself up for me."

And so it must be with you. You live your human life, but you live it in faith in Christ Jesus.

Those first two readings, along with the responsorial psalm, give you your bearings. Forgiveness, given to David and available to you, is plainly there. Faith, your life of faith in the Son of God, is brought before your consciousness. And you are reminded that it was love that prompted Christ to give himself for you. Thus, the stage is set for you to observe the encounter of Jesus and the sinful woman.

45

Twelfth Sunday of the Year

Self-Denial, Cross Carrying, and Discipleship

Zechariah 12:10–11; Psalm 63; Galatians 3:26–29; Luke 9:18–24

There is a story told about U.S. Confederate General Robert E. Lee that is documented at the end of the last volume in the four-volume biography of Lee written by Douglas Freeman. The biographer notes that if you wanted to sum up the entire life of Robert E. Lee, you would have to go to "the Book"—the Bible—that meant so much to Lee and turn to the lines that you just heard in today's Gospel reading: Jesus said to all: "If anyone wishes to come after me, he must deny himself and take up his cross daily and follow me." (Luke 9:23)

And Douglas Freeman added that if you wanted an incident in the life of Lee that illustrates this point, he would invite you back to a small Northern Virginia town that Lee and some of his officers approached one day on horseback. When word spread that General Lee was nearing the town and would be riding through, people came out of their houses and lined the road in order to get a better glimpse of him passing by. A young mother went to the side of the road holding her infant son in her arms. When General Lee drew near, she raised her son up and asked the General to "bless" her baby. Lee stopped his horse, reached down to touch the head of the infant, looked the mother in the eye and said to her, "Teach him he must deny himself."

It is hard for us to imagine a contemporary military general being asked to bless a child. It is even harder, perhaps, in our day, to look upon self-denial as a blessing and not a curse. In any case, that is what Lee said and that is how, historians say, Lee lived.

Our Church is inviting all of us today to consider these rather stern words of Jesus addressed to anyone who wishes to be his disciple. The instruction is clear. Practice self-denial. Take up your cross. Follow in the footsteps of Jesus. If you walk the way he walked, you'll find yourself walking the way of the cross.

Self-denial does not mean self-denigration or self-hatred. It really means self-control. Carrying the cross does not always mean bearing the full weight; it might be just putting up with splinters from time to time. But it does mean that Jesus saw redemptive power in hardships—as mysterious as they may be—and that in following him, you will walk through defeat to victory, through death to life. This is a mystery—the Paschal Mystery—and it is a way of life for the Christian.

Now surely and certainly there is joy in the Christian life, there is happiness, much happiness. There will be many good times; there will be lots of fun. But integral to the Christian life, the life of Christian discipleship, is the cross. You must never ignore it, or take it for granted, or regard it as a piece of jewelry, an ornament, or work of art. The cross represents harsh reality in the life of the Christian. It is full of mystery. And it will always be there.

The cross serves to remind that there is something countercultural in the life of the Christian. The "good life" for the Christian is not a life without reversals, without sorrow or suffering. You can't pretend that suffering is not there or will never be there. It is sure to come. But this also is sure: If you deny yourself and carry your cross, you will find yourself and you will experience deep happiness in this world and eternal happiness in the world to come.

My father died at age 32. He died of a duodenal ulcer that ruptured. No one would die of that today. He was a physician but, unfortunately for him, he died before his profession produced the antibiotics that would have restored him to health. He left behind a wife, my mother, also 32, and two infant children—my brother, age two-and-a-half, and I, seven months old. I never knew him. I was well into adulthood and a priest for twenty years or more when I received a letter from a retired nun whom I did not know. She saw some mention of me in a news article and wrote to explain that as a very young nun she was assigned to teach in the parochial school in the parish where I grew up. She remembered, she wrote, seeing my mother making the Stations of the Cross after Mass in our parish church with two young toddlers in tow. I have no memory at all of that. And, she said, she was so impressed by the devotion, faith, and commitment exhibited by my young mother, that she was both edified and strengthened in her own vocational commitment. She was more sure-footed in walking her own way of the cross because she watched my mother walking hers.

Jesus began the lesson that he offers you in today's Gospel with a question to his disciples: "Who do the crowds say that I am?" That's a good question for each of you to turn around on yourselves. Take a moment to do that today. Who do you say he is? Who is Jesus to you at this point in your life? What is the meaning of Jesus—directly and personally—to you? You don't have to have a mental picture of him. If you do, that's fine; but it is not necessary. You should, however, have an impression of him, an idea of him as a person and power within you. He is your friend. He knows you. He loves you. And somehow, somewhere, woven into that impression you have of Jesus, you should have that notion of Savior, you should include the dimension of suffering because that is what he did, that is who he was and is for you. And that is why he, ever so gently but also clearly, can make a demand on you, as he does in today's Gospel: "If anyone wishes to come after me, he must deny himself and take up his cross daily and follow me. For whoever wishes to save his life will lose it, but whoever loses his life for my sake will save it."

So there you are. The choice is yours. But remember, he is your friend who wants nothing but the best for you. Follow him and you will never lose your way.

46

Thirteenth Sunday of the Year

Stand Firm; You Were Called to Freedom

1 Kings 19:16b, 19–21; Psalm 16; Galatians 5:1, 13–18; Luke 9:51–62

"Stand firm," Paul tells the Galatians in this morning's second reading. "For freedom Christ set us free; so stand firm and do not submit again to the yoke of slavery."

Each one of you can hear those words directed to yourself today, dear friends: Stand firm; for you were called to freedom. Some of us don't know how to handle freedom. Some of us prefer to use authority as a substitute for personal decision making and personal responsibility. "Is it all right," you ask, "if I do this or that?" "Well," I might say to you in reply, "what do you think? Do what you think is right." And, if you do not handle freedom comfortably, you might not be happy with that reply.

There is another external factor that undermines that "firmness" that we who are free should know and celebrate in our lives. That external factor is technology and the accidents or collisions that result from failed technology. Is there going to be a power outage? Will my computer crash? Will I lose my memory (not because of Alzheimer's, but because of power failures and inadequate backup provisions)? Will a manhole cover blow up into the air as I walk along a city street or enter a shopping center? Will there be another Three Mile Island? Will the air traffic controller forget that my plane is about to cross a busy runway? Is there a terrorist attack about to happen?

We seem to find ourselves in a culture of contingency—job loss, broken promises, sudden death. We hesitate to make commitments. We unwittingly adopt an approach to life that is characterized by hesitation. So it is good to hear Paul say to us today, "Stand firm; you were called to freedom." And it is good for us to consider how we might use our freedom responsibly and well. That will happen if we adopt an additional piece of the advice offered by Paul to the Galatians: "Live by the Spirit and you will certainly not gratify the desire of the flesh. For the flesh has desires against the Spirit, and the Spirit against the flesh; these are opposed to each other, so that you may not do what you want."

Not do what I want? How then am I free? I am free, Paul would say, only when I "live by the Spirit" and am "guided by the Spirit." And how might I know whether or not I'm living by the Spirit and under the guidance of the Spirit? You have to read on in the fifth chapter of Paul's Letter to the Galatians, the chapter from which this morning's excerpt is taken. Do that when you return home today and you'll notice that Paul identifies the "fruit" of the Spirit—evidence or signs that the Spirit is present in a person or a place. How can you tell whether the Spirit is there within you or around you? Look for these nine characteristics, these nine qualities that make up what Paul calls the "fruit" of the Spirit. If they are there, the Holy Spirit is there. If they are absent, then you have to wonder.

Love, joy, peace, patience, kindness, generosity, faithfulness, gentleness, and self-control. There they are. Possess those and you are free. Possess those and you are in possession of the Holy Spirit and you can indeed "stand firm" and enjoy your freedom.

Today's Gospel passage from St. Luke begins with the fifty-first verse of Luke's ninth chapter. This is a famous mile marker in the public life of Jesus. For it is at Luke 9:51 where the account of Jesus' life puts him on the road to Jerusalem. He will not return. He is heading directly to death and glorification. Listen again: "When the days for his being taken up were fulfilled, he resolutely determined to journey to Jerusalem."

Resolutely. He will not turn back. He determined—he chose freely— to journey to Jerusalem. No need to say much more about this today. It will be sufficient for you to turn that adverb "resolutely" over in your mind and heart. Resolute. That was Jesus. That should be you. How can you "stand firm" and not be resolute? How can you live as a man or woman "called to freedom" and not be concerned to "live by the Spirit," nor be anxious to be "guided by the Spirit?"

Be firm, be free, be flexible, be resolute, be Christian. And follow your Master on your own personal journey to Jerusalem.

47

Fourteenth Sunday of the Year

"Like Lambs Among Wolves"

Isaiah 68:10–14c; Psalm 66; Galatians 6:14–18; Luke 10:1–12, 17–20

Today's Gospel reminds you of your call to discipleship, your call to be ambassadors for Christ; it reminds you of your vocation to spread the good news of salvation. By an act of your imagination put yourself in that long line of seventy-two whom Jesus sent out in pairs "to every town and place he intended to visit." You can imagine that he called each of them by name and expressed his gratitude to them as he encouraged them to prepare the way for him. He invites you now to do exactly that in your own sphere of influence, in your own towns and workplaces.

Jesus outlined for the seventy-two, and for you as well, a strategy of gentleness—gentle persistence, you might call it. He said to them, "Into whatever house you enter, first, say 'Peace to this household.'" And he also instructed his ambassadors, his advance squad, if you will, that he wanted them to proceed "like lambs among wolves." They would surely meet opposition, but that should neither surprise nor deter them. They should travel light and be patiently and gently persistent in extending a greeting of peace. If their peace is rejected, they should not be deterred. They can simply shake the dust of an unreceptive town from their feet and move on. Their message, followed by a greeting of peace, is always the same: "The kingdom of God is at hand for you."

The task of evangelization would take them, and you, into hostile territory where there will be resistance if not outright rejection of God's reign, rejection of God's plan that human wills should be aligned with his divine will. And what is it that God wills? The prophet Micah said it quite well: "You have been told, O mortal, what is good, and what the Lord requires of you: Only to do justice and to love goodness, and to walk humbly with your God" (6:8). That's a fair description of the reign of God. Once men and women worldwide choose to act justly, to love tenderly, and to walk humbly with their God, the promised reign or kingdom of God will have come. As disciples and ambassadors for Christ, each one of us has a responsibility to do what we can to prepare the way for the coming of that promised kingdom.

Justice, love, and peace; fair dealings with one another, attentive care for one another, and humble submission to God's will—that is what each of us should be proclaiming in both word and example, especially in example. You know the old saying: "What you do speaks to me so loudly I can hardly hear what you say." So do justice; do indeed love one another, and let others see you walking humbly with your God. Just do all that. Others will surely notice and, by God's grace, may even do likewise.

Notice that the seventy-two in this Gospel story "returned rejoicing, and said, 'Lord, even the demons are subject to us because of your name.'" They hadn't yet changed the world, but they did make some progress. The hostile forces, the opposition, did not do them in. They felt pretty good about that and by their "rejoicing" they reinforced one another in their commitment to Christ and the objectives of his kingdom. We need that kind of reinforcement today in these modern times as we work with one another for Christ in his work, so much of which remains to be done. Just look around you at the greed and graft, the corruption and exploitation, the violence and lust, the sheer evil in your world and you'll have a measure of the extent to which the work of Christ—the peace, love, justice agenda—remains to be done. You cannot let yourself become complacent in the midst of evil, but neither can you permit yourself to grow discouraged. Return from time to time "rejoicing" to your Master—particularly at times like this in the Eucharistic liturgy—and recommit yourselves to the task of discipleship.

Jesus mysteriously said to them, as he may well be saying to you today, "I have observed Satan fall like lightening from the sky." You are not likely to see that. But you should know that Satan is out there and that the forces of Satan are aligned against you. Moreover, you should know that Satan can be overcome and that Jesus is counting on you and will be with you in your efforts to counter the forces of evil in your world.

Remember that you are lambs in the midst of wolves. That's the way Jesus wanted it. And as the second reading the Church offers for your consideration today, the selection from Paul's Letter to the Galatians, puts it: "But may I never boast except in the cross of our Lord Jesus Christ, through which the world has been crucified to me, and I to the world.... From now on, let no one make troubles for me; for I bear the marks of Jesus on my body." This is inspired Scripture, the word of God. This is a reminder that you live and work under the banner of the cross. You are indeed "lambs in the midst of wolves" but the brand marks of Jesus on your body are both badges of honor and protective armor in the war you've been called to wage—gently and peaceably, to be sure—with the forces of evil in your world.

48

Fifteenth Sunday of the Year

"What Must I Do to Inherit Eternal Life?"

Deuteronomy 30:10–14; Psalm 69; Colossians 1:15–20;
Luke 10:25–37

The lawyer in today's Gospel story raises a good question, one that is worthy of more than casual consideration on the part of each one of us. He says to Jesus, "Teacher, what must I do to inherit eternal life?" And notice that the answer to this question features the notion of neighbor—who is your neighbor, how do you treat your neighbor?

First, however, Jesus asks the lawyer to review the law of what is required of all of us to make it home to heaven. "What is written in the law?" asks Jesus; "How do you read it [the law]?" And the inquiring lawyer replied by ticking off the "great commandments" as they were given to Moses: "You shall love the Lord, your God, with all your heart, with all your being, with all your strength, and with all your mind; and your neighbor as yourself." But then the lawyer asked, "And who is my neighbor?" And this question opens the door to one of the most famous stories in all of literature, the so-called parable of the Good Samaritan that has come down to us through the centuries and is so familiar to each one of you.

It is a story noted for its simplicity. The traveler is making his way from Jericho to Jerusalem; he falls in with robbers, they strip him, mug him, and walk off leaving him half dead. A priest comes along the same road, sees the victim, and continues on his way. Similarly, a Levite passes by. Then along comes a Samaritan—the ethnic identification is important because Jews and Samaritans did not get along; Jews, in fact, discriminated against Samaritans. And here you see a generous Samaritan who stops to help a half-dead Jew. This would be analogous to a Mississippi black man several generations ago stopping to assist a member of the Ku Klux Klan. The Gospel story relates it this way:

171

"But a Samaritan traveler who came upon him [the victim] was moved with compassion at the sight. He approached the victim, poured oil and wine over his wounds, and bandaged them. Then he lifted him up on his own animal, took him to an inn and cared for him."

How often have you seen a Good Samaritan Hospital in a modern city? How often have you read or heard about a "Good Samaritan Law" that addresses liability issues relating to cases of roadside assistance for victims of attack or accident? The notion of a Good Samaritan is universally known and understood. But what is often forgotten is that this notion found its way into human discourse through a story told by Jesus to explain the meaning of "neighbor."

After bringing the victim to an inn, the Samaritan tells the innkeeper to look after the man and whatever expense is incurred will be covered by the Samaritan when he returns. Let me remark that the innkeeper deserves his share of credit in this story. The Good Samaritan moved on and the innkeeper was left to meet immediate care-giving responsibilities. No small demand was being made upon him. In any case, Jesus ends the story by asking: "Which of these three [the priest, Levite, or the Samaritan traveler]... was neighbor to the robbers' victim?" And, of course, "He answered, 'The one who treated him with mercy.'" And the story closes with words from Jesus spoken not only to the inquiring lawyer but down through the centuries to each one of us: "Go and do likewise."

There you have it. A classic story; a profound moral lesson. And notice that all of this is directly related to the issue of your salvation: "Teacher, what must I do to inherit eternal life?" is the question that triggered the story in the first place. Let me point out the significance of the word "inherit." The question does not speak of "meriting" or "earning," but simply of being eligible to receive a gift you don't deserve, a gift beyond measuring, an inheritance of inestimable worth. So add a dimension of gratitude to your reflection on the relevance of the Samaritan story to yourself. Be grateful for your inheritance.

And there is no escaping your responsibility, as you reflect on the implications of this story for yourself today, to be compassionate and to be aware of your neighbor who may not live in what you regard as your neighborhood, in your zip code; who may not have much in common with you (except the common human nature, which you both share), who may not speak your language, share your ethnicity, nor look anything like someone you would typically want to associate with, yet is nonetheless your neighbor! That unnoticed neighbor may be in need of help. Without your compassionate response that neighbor may die.

So if everyone in your circle of friends looks, and talks, and thinks exactly as you do, you have to pause for a few reflective moments and wonder whether something of the insensitive, uncaring, and unresponsive priest or Levite resides in you. And you would do well today to take another look at the headlines and see if there are references there to neighbors you have not noticed—immigrants, for example, experiencing difficulty finding acceptance here in the United States; people in Africa suffering from AIDS; refugees; the hungry; those who are in prison. You have a lot of neighbors who are in need; some are nearby, some are far away. They are in need of your prayers. They are in need for your helping hand. They are in need of your charitable contributions. Those who are literally within sight and within reach might be considered to have first claim on your attention. But you have to first begin noticing them. You have to face up to the question Sacred Scripture raised centuries ago through the voice of the lawyer asking Jesus. "And who is my neighbor?"

Your answer to that question will be aided by the story of the Good Samaritan. And your reaction to the story of the Good Samaritan should begin by heeding the injunction Jesus gave to those who heard it from him for the first time centuries ago: now "go and do likewise."

49

Sixteenth Sunday of the Year

Martha and Mary

Genesis 18:1–10; Psalm 15; Colossians 1:24–28; Luke 10:38–42

I have a long-time friend whose name is Martha, although everyone calls her Martie. She tells me that this Gospel story was a familiar one around her home as she was growing up with two sisters with whom she frequently debated the fairness of the allocation of household chores, particularly the task of cleaning up after dinner. Her brothers were mute auditors of these discussions back in the days when male members of the family where not held responsible for kitchen cleanup. But the relative responsibilities of Martha and Mary, about which Jesus had something to say in this Gospel account, were and still are topics of conversation in many Christian families. My sister-in-law's name is Marta—Marta Gonzalez Byron. She is the mother of eight. Her kitchen was decorated with many humorous reminders that household tasks were meant to be spread around— that she was not the hired hand.

It is interesting to note that the famous Dutch artist Rembrandt (1606–1669) chose the biblical story of Martha and Mary as the subject for several pieces of his pen-and-brown-ink-on-paper religious art. In one instance, he purposely smears or "washes" the figure of Martha, as if to highlight her harried activity in contrast to the clear ink depiction of Jesus and Martha's sister Mary sitting quietly at table. And in at least two of his renderings of this biblical scene, Rembrandt has Mary reading a book as if to add the studious to the contemplative dimension of her character.

You are all familiar with the story. Martha was the one who welcomed Jesus to their home. Martha had a sister Mary "[who] sat beside the Lord at his feet listening to him speak" as Martha was "burdened with much serving." Famously, Martha spoke up to Jesus and complained, "Lord, do you not care that my sister has left me by myself to do the serving? Tell her to help me." To Martha's surprise, I suspect, Jesus replied to her complaint by reminding her that there are two sides to the Christian life—the active and the contemplative—and that Mary "has chosen the better part and it will not be taken from her."

Over the centuries, there's been no little debate in the Catholic world about the relative merits of the active religious life over against the vocation to contemplative life. Who has the higher calling—the active Jesuit priest or the prayerful Trappist monk, the Carmelite nun in her monastery or the Sister of Mercy in her hospital or classroom? There's not much point in engaging in that debate now because the only calling that is important is the one God directs toward you. Be what God calls you to be; that's what is best for you. That is what is "highest" for you. Similarly, the lay life—"in the world," as we say—if that's where you are called to be, that is what is highest and best for you.

Reflection on the story of Martha and Mary presents all of us with an opportunity to give some thought to balance in our lives, particularly, the balance between the active and contemplative dimensions of our spiritual lives. Prayer is important—not just liturgical prayer or the prayer of petition, but the quiet prayer of contemplation. We tend to neglect the demands of the quiet side in favor of the hyperactive, being-busy-about-a-lot-of-things side of our religious lives. Our response to the Christ who calls us to be Christian, to follow Christ, to offer him our voice, our hands, and our feet to go about doing his work here on earth—our response is a tendency to get up and go. We want to be on the move. We want to be busy about a lot of things. In other words, we want to be like Martha.

But here you have Jesus saying that Mary has chosen the better part—to sit at his feet, to quietly contemplate, to listen to him. And, if Rembrandt is to be believed, Jesus expects you to read a book or two to get the mind engaged.

The trouble with the world, someone once remarked, is that most of the active people never think and most of the thinkers never act. We need both—thought and action—in all areas of life. And it is to the point that this Gospel story raises for our consideration today to say that each one of us should have a proper balance of action and contemplation in his or her personal Christian life. That sounds just a bit strange—all right, but strange nonetheless, to speak of a "personal" Christian life. Every life that is lived in Christ is lived in his body. We used to speak of the Mystical Body of Christ as a description of the Church; it was understood to include all the baptized, all those who have put on Christ in baptism and who are nourished by the body and blood of Christ, who have become one body in the Eucharist. You and I and all other believers make up the one body of Christ. And we bring Christ to the world.

I've always been fond of this reflection attributed to St. Teresa of Avila:

Christ has no body on earth but

yours; no hands on earth but your hands,

no feet on earth but yours.

Yours are the eyes through

which he looks with compassion on

the world; yours are the feet with

which he walks about doing good; yours

are the hands with which he blesses

all the world.

Christ has no body

now on the earth but yours.

The question for us all is what are we doing practically and apostolically with our eyes, hands, feet, and our minds as well; what are we doing to train our hearts, hands, minds, and eyes to be available to and useful to Christ to serve his purposes in his world and ours today? What would Christ have us do today with our hands and minds? We'll never know unless we quiet down, go apart, stop chattering and begin to listen to the God who holds us in his hand, the God who calls us to serve one another, the God who depends, however mysteriously, on us to get to work for him in this world.

If you lean toward action, don't neglect contemplation. If you prefer solitude, don't remain disengaged from the fray. Work, by God's grace, for balance in your life. Let both Martha and Mary come alive in you for the glory of God and the good of the human community.

50

Seventeenth Sunday of the Year

"Lord, Teach Us to Pray"

Genesis 18:20–32; Psalm 138; Colossians 2:12–14; Luke 11:1–13

"Lord, teach us to pray..." Any one of you could have asked that "how-to-pray" question of your Lord. Luke reports in today's Gospel account that one of the disciples of Jesus, an unnamed follower of Christ, asked the Lord for instruction in prayer and the answer that disciple received is heard today and every day throughout the world. "When you pray, say: Father, hallowed be your name, / your kingdom come. / Give us each day our daily bread / and forgive us our sins / for we ourselves forgive everyone in debt to us / and do not subject us to the final test."

"Lord, teach us to pray."

You can learn from the response of Jesus to that request that your prayer should have an element of awe—"hallowed be your name." Your prayer puts you in the holy presence, the awesome presence of God. Be calm there. Be at peace. Don't multiply words. Be gratefully aware of God's presence to you. "Hallowed be your name." Begin there, in reverence, in God's presence.

And when you pray, be sure to say, "your kingdom come." Your prayer must be apostolic. It should display a concern for the coming of God's kingdom of justice, love, and peace. It should reflect an uneasiness, a discontent, with injustice in any form, with hatred of any kind, with conflict of any intensity. "Your kingdom come" is a plea that God will hasten the arrival of his reign of justice, love, and peace, and that we humans will lower and eventually remove the obstacles we place in the way of the coming kingdom.

"Lord, teach us to pray."

You will notice that the instruction Jesus gives you on prayer includes a conscious expression of your dependency on God's providence for your basic needs. How easy it is in an advanced, affluent, technologically strong society to forget our dependency on God. So pray, and mean what you pray, in the words Jesus gave you: "Give us each day our daily bread."

Think for a moment about bread in your life—your daily bread. Think of the bread of life, the Eucharist. Think of the bread for life, the bread on your table. There is a lovely anonymous Scottish verse (its author is unknown) that you might consider:

Be gentle when you touch bread

Let it not lie uncared for, unwanted.

There is so much beauty in bread,

Beauty of sun and soil.

Beauty of patient toil

Winds and rain have caressed it,

Christ so often blessed it.

Be gentle when you touch bread.

Now, Lord, teach us still more about prayer. And the Lord responds to that request by reminding you to pray for forgiveness. "And forgive us our sins," as the translation before us this morning puts it, "for we ourselves forgive everyone in debt to us." Oh, do we? Or do we hold grudges, make unusual demands, press or even oppress the weak?

Lord, teach us not only to pray, teach us to forgive, and teach us that we must forgive if our prayer is to be heard by you. Quite understandably, we may find it humanly impossible to forget when we've been wronged, but we can, by God's grace, find it within ourselves to forgive!

"And do not subject us to the final test." What might that mean? We know we will be judged. We always hope that somehow or other we will be able to skip the final exam and still exit the course with a passing grade. What the Lord would have us pray for here in this more familiar "lead us not into temptation" clause, is for spiritual strength to overcome our spiritual enemies, the enemy (singular) of our human nature (and that, of course, is Satan); we are praying here for protection against the forces of evil. It is foolish for us to live as if there were no evil in the world, as though no traps had been set for us, as if God's enemies had no interest in us, the people of God.

After the recitation here in Luke's Gospel of what Luke records as The Lord's Prayer, Jesus teaches us about another important element in prayer, namely, persistence. "And he said to them, 'Suppose one of you has a friend to whom he goes at midnight and says, 'Friend, lend me three loaves of bread, for a friend of mine has arrived at my house from a journey and I have nothing to offer him,' and he says in reply from within, 'Do not bother me; the door has already been locked and my children and I are already in bed. I cannot get up and give you anything.' I tell you [says Jesus], if he does not get up to give the visitor the loaves because of their friendship, he will get up to give him whatever he needs because of his persistence." That fellow in need of bread is going to keep on knocking and calling out for help!

So be not only faithful to prayer, but persistent in prayer, especially the prayer of petition. In thinking about your prayer of petition, recall the familiar image from summers past when you were on a lake, in a boat, and the boat drew near to the dock. You threw out a line and it caught on a cleat at the edge of the dock, and you pulled yourself in. You didn't pull the dock toward you; you pulled yourself toward the dock. That's the way it works with the prayer of petition. You toss up and out your prayer, your request, and it catches onto a heavenly "cleat," so to speak. God hears you. But you don't pull God toward you (even though you may think you can by your pleading!), any more than you could pull the dock toward your boat. No, you are drawn toward God, disposed to accept what God regards as best for you. Your prayer of petition disposes you, readies you, to receive what God wants you to have; it doesn't pull God toward your way of thinking or "bend" God's will to yours. You always know that the answer to your specific request might be, "no," even though something different and better will indeed come your way.

"Ask and you will receive; seek and you will find; knock and the door will be opened to you." They are not my words; they are the words of Jesus Christ recorded in this Gospel and speaking directly to you today. Take him at his word. Keep on asking. Keep on seeking. Keep on knocking. God will never ignore you, disappoint you, or let you down.

51

Eighteenth Sunday of the Year

"Take Care to Guard Against Greed"

Ecclesiastes 1:2, 2:21–23; Psalm 90; Colossians 3:1–5, 9–11;
Luke 12:13–21

Jesus has good advice to offer you in today's Gospel: "Take care to guard against all greed." He offers this advice in a context provided first by some wisdom from the Book of Ecclesiastes, famous for its "vanity of vanities" warnings. In that first reading you heard that "All things are vanity!" A strong statement, presumably looking toward the material things we tend to accumulate and fret about losing. Eventually all your material possessions will be left behind. So it is simply foolish to act now as if they will always be yours.

That's the point of the story Jesus tells in the Gospel reading you just heard about the rich man who had a good harvest and wondered how he would store it. He hit upon the idea of tearing down his present barn, his existing grain bins, and then building larger ones. "There I shall store all my grain and other goods," says the man, "and I shall say to myself, 'Now as for you, you have so many good things stored up for many years, rest, eat, drink, be merry!'" But it seems that God had other plans. The Gospel story tells you: "But God said to him, 'You fool, this night your life will be demanded of you; and the things you have prepared, to whom will they belong?'"

All this comes from the lips of Jesus, not from some protesting demonstrator or social critic. Jesus, speaking to you for your own good, points out that there can be problems for you—big problems—associated with piled-up wealth—wealth not shared, wealth coveted and hoarded, wealth with the potential to smother, even choke, the one who hangs onto it.

Throughout his public life Jesus warned people not to be possessed by their possessions. He never said that things—possessions—were in themselves bad. But he did suggest that attachment to the things of this world could become addictive and even destructive.

Let me come at this from another angle. There is a role in God's providence for saints—like Ignatius of Loyola—to rephrase Gospel wisdom and convey it in ways that ordinary believers might more easily grasp. Let me give you an example that may help you better understand this Gospel message.

Ignatius had a tendency to see life as a struggle between the forces of good and the forces of evil. He was a mystic who saw the world from God's point of view. He founded his religious order for like-minded men called, as he was, to be contemplatives in action. Ignatius and his first companions committed themselves "to travel anywhere in the world where there is hope of God's greater glory and the good of souls." The initials "A.M.D.G." and the phrase, "God's greater glory," appear on the logo or "coat of arms," of many Jesuit institutions and organizations. The Jesuit motto, "Ad Maiorem Dei Gloriam" suggests that Ignatius would have you always looking higher—to the greater good of others and to the greater glory of God. *"More"*—not "the most" in any acquisitive sense—but "more," "the magis," is the Ignatian way to meet any challenge with a fuller stretch of effort and talent.

In his book of *Spiritual Exercises*, a retreat handbook or outline intended to guide one's prayer in the quest for a better understanding of God's will, there is a special Meditation on Two Standards (*Spiritual Exercises*, 136ff.), *"the one of Christ, our Supreme Commander and Lord, the other of Lucifer, the mortal enemy of our human nature."* (A "standard," as used here, is a military banner or "guide on" employed to lead forces in battle.) The following paragraphs, excerpted from that meditation, pertain to the Standard of Christ (*Spiritual Exercises*, 145–146). Ignatius states that "Christ calls and desires all persons to come under his standard," and then invites the retreatant, in an exercise of the imagination, to place him- or herself in the presence of Christ and listen.

> Consider the address which Christ our Lord makes to all his servants and friends whom he is sending on this expedition. He recommends that they endeavor to aid all persons, by attracting them, first, to the

most perfect spiritual poverty and also, if the Divine Majesty should
be served and should wish to choose them for it, even to no less a
degree of actual poverty; and second, by attracting them to a desire for
reproaches and contempt, since from these results humility.

In this way there will be three steps: the first, poverty in opposition
to riches; the second, reproaches or contempt in opposition to honor
from the world; and the third, humility in opposition to pride. Then
from these three steps they should induce people to all the other
virtues.

The Standard of Christ offers this clearly counter-cultural insight or
wisdom principle: The three steps to genuine success are poverty as
opposed to riches; insults or contempt as opposed to the honor of this
world; humility as opposed to pride. "From these three steps let them
lead men to all other virtues." (*Spiritual Exercises,* 146).

It was remarked in 2008 by Jesuit Cardinal Carlos Martini that delivery of the *Spiritual Exercises,* particularly the proclamation of the
Standard of Christ, is "the service that the Society of Jesus is called
to perform for the Church today." To the completely secular eye, that
will be seen as no service at all. To the eye of faith, acceptance of the
genuine Ignatian vision and values will be seen as a form of liberation.
That's why I am offering this for your consideration now.

There are, according to St. Ignatius, three levels of alignment of
one's will with the will of God. The first is necessary for salvation. "I
so subject and humble myself as to obey the law of God our Lord
in all things" (*Spiritual Exercises,* 165). This level of humility is thus
understood as obedience to God's will. The second kind or degree of
humility means "that I neither desire nor am I inclined to have riches
rather than poverty, to seek honor rather than dishonor, to desire a
long life rather than a short life, provided only in either alternative I
would promote equally the service of God our Lord and the salvation
of my soul" (*Spiritual Exercises,* 166). This is what is known as Ignatian
"indifference"—humility thus understood eliminates one's personal
desire as finally decisive and determinative. The third or highest degree

of humility implies the desire to be like Christ who is poor, despised, and deemed foolish.

This third is a high level or degree of sanctity—a goal to be sought, a condition to be valued. Ignatius says that the one making the Exercises "should beg our Lord to deign to choose him [or her] for this kind of humility...provided equal praise and service be given to the Divine Majesty" (*Spiritual Exercises*, 168).

The Ignatian wisdom principle that is relevant here is that humility, as demonstrated in the life of Christ, is a useful guideline for following the injunction Jesus gave to avoid greed in all its forms.

The Standard of Satan, according to Ignatius, represents a three-step strategy intended to trap the unwary and lead them away from Christ and into perdition. To ignore this warning is sheer folly.

In order to enable the retreatant to consider the Standard of Satan, Ignatius would have him or her "see the chief of all the enemy in the vast plain about Babylon, seated on a great throne of fire and smoke, his appearance inspiring horror and terror" (*Spiritual Exercises*, 140). Then Ignatius would have the retreatant "consider how [Satan] summons innumerable demons, and scatters them, some to one city and some to another, throughout the whole world, so that no province, no place, no state of life, no individual is overlooked." And finally, Ignatius would ask those who put themselves in prayer in this way to "consider the address [Satan] makes to them [the demons], how he goads them on to lay snares for men, to seek to chain them. First they are to tempt them to covet riches (as Satan himself is accustomed to do in most cases) that they may the more easily attain the empty honors of this world, and then come to overweening pride. The first step, then, will be riches, the second honor, the third pride. From these three steps the evil one leads to all other vices" (*Spiritual Exercises*, 142).

Obviously, there is a viewpoint that is shaped by the *Spiritual Exercises* and it is clearly countercultural. When John Kenneth Galbraith's landmark book *The Affluent Society* was making the rounds in the late 1950s, the author's comments about the "basic benefits" of having wealth reflected the values of the dominant culture, but they also struck an unintended echo of the Standard of Satan. Here is what Galbraith wrote: "Broadly speaking, there are three basic benefits from wealth. First, is the satisfaction in the power with which it endows the individual. Second is the physical possession of the things which money can buy. Third is the distinction or esteem that accrues to the rich man as a result of his wealth" [*The Affluent Society* (Houghton Mifflin, 1958, p. 88)].

The power-possession-esteem triad echoes the strategy Ignatius saw as the trap set by the enemy of our human nature.

Returning now to today's Gospel story, it is evident that the rich man who wanted to tear down his barns and build bigger ones had no idea that he was caught in a trap set by the enemy of his human nature. The prospect of wallowing in his possessions, of relaxing, eating and drinking well—all forms of greed—dominated his mind. He was buried by "piled-up wealth" and didn't even know it.

So listen to Jesus when he speaks to you today and warns you to avoid greed in all its forms. Happily, your number will in all probability not be up tomorrow, but you will have an opportunity then to reflect on the strategy of Satan and consider the wisdom represented by the Standard of Christ. Riches, honor, and pride can do you in; poverty, reproaches, and humility can be your salvation!

52

Nineteenth Sunday of the Year

A Threat or a Promise?

Wisdom 18:6–9; Psalm 33; Hebrews 11:1–2, 8–19; Luke 12:32–48

There are several ways in which you can react to this Gospel message. I will offer you a choice. You can view it as a promise; or you can take it as a threat, or at least as a warning.

You heard Jesus say: "You also must be prepared, for at an hour you do not expect the Son of Man will come." Is that a promise or a warning? To some extent your answer to that question depends on how you view Jesus. Is Jesus your friend—showing up from time to time to give you grace and encouragement? Is he there, wanting to make his presence felt, and might you be missing him—distracted, inattentive? He is promising to be there for you. Don't neglect him; don't run the risk of missing him. The Son of Man will come when you are not expecting him.

Or do you have a view of Jesus that makes him out to be an investigator and judge, perhaps even a police presence in your life. He'll nail you, if you are not careful. So be on the lookout; you might get caught! The way you react to this saying of Jesus that the Son of Man will come when you least expect him, depends in no small measure on the way you regard the Lord and the way you regard yourself. It's your choice.

You also heard Jesus say in today's Gospel: "Gird your loins and light your lamps, and be like servants who await their master's return." This is a call to readiness—is it a threat or a promise? Are you confidently ready to receive more of his love and grace, or are you nervously ready to avoid being caught in an action, situation, or state of mind where you should not be? Are you driven by joy or fear, by grace or guilt?

Jesus goes on to say: "Be like servants who await their master's return from a wedding, ready to open immediately when he comes and knocks." Strange, isn't it? That the master would have to knock to gain entrance. It is, after all, his home. Why would he have to knock? Why couldn't he just walk right in? There is a suggestion here of an exquisite courtesy on the part of Jesus as he approaches each one of us. He won't just break in on you uninvited; he won't impose himself on you. No forced entry. You have to be ready and willing; you have to be open to his divine initiatives toward you. You have to want him.

Moreover, the Gospel story indicates that the master will be pleased if he finds his servants busy upon his return, so much so that he will "gird himself, have them recline at table, and proceed to wait on them." What an unusual picture that is! Your Lord and master is willing to be your servant. Not all that surprising, however, when you pause to think about it. He did, after all, wash his disciples' feet at the Last Supper. He is standing by, always, ready to wash yours. Don't back away with an exaggerated sense of your own unworthiness. He is your friend. He wants to help. He wants to be close to you. Just accept that fact. Enjoy his friendship, his presence.

Reflection on your own personal reaction to the words of Jesus in today's Gospel is a healthy exercise. Most of us tend to harbor an unhealthy negative estimate of our own worth. Yes, I know we are encouraged to say, "Lord I am not worthy" as we approach the Communion encounter with Christ at Mass. That is all good and true. But all too often we regard ourselves not just as unworthy, but as worthless. The others around me—to the right or left, in front or behind—they are fine; they are good and deserving of the Lord's love. But not me. I'm no good.

That is a terrible temptation. Face up to it. Confront it head on and just say, "Begone Satan. Get out of here. Stop lying to me. Stop trying to convince me that God doesn't love me. God does indeed love me; I know that by faith."

So let me suggest that you listen again to the opening words of the second reading in today's liturgy, the selection you heard read from the Letter to the Hebrews (11:1): "Faith is the realization of what is hoped for, and evidence of things not seen." Have faith in yourself as well as in God. Certainly your faith in yourself is related to your faith in God, but notice how hope is tied in with your acceptance of the gift of faith.

There is much that is real in life that we cannot see, but it is real nonetheless.

And the point to be stressed today is the reality of God's love for you, God's presence to you, God's care for you. You will be tempted not to believe this. You will be tempted to think that God does not really care about you, or you may be tricked into thinking that God is all threat and no promise, that God sees you only so that he can condemn you, not because he delights in seeing you, and loving you, and sustaining you by his always available forgiveness and healing grace.

Satan is at work in the world. He is the enemy of our human nature. His demons are scattered around the globe and their aim is to substitute hate for love, evil for good, and to separate the human race from God. Not one of us is overlooked. Each one of us can expect to be tempted. And for many of us that temptation will come in the form of self-hatred, self-distrust, an erosion of self-confidence and a deafness to the knock of Christ on our doors as well as a blindness to the presence of Christ in our daily lives.

"You also must be prepared, for at an hour you do not expect, the Son of Man will come." He is there right now. Recognize him, Welcome him. Accept his forgiveness and grace. Follow him wherever he leads.

53

Twentieth Sunday of the Year

"I Have Come to Set the Earth on Fire"

Jeremiah 38:4–6, 8–10; Psalm 40; Hebrews 12:1–4; Luke 12:49–53

The readings from Scripture that the Church asks us to reflect upon today are, generally speaking, difficult to relate to one another, indeed difficult to understand. The prophet Jeremiah is saved from death in a cistern. The responsorial psalm puts a cry for help on our lips: "Lord, come to my aid!" The selection from the Letter to the Hebrews that we have as a second reading offers good advice: "Let us rid ourselves of every burden and sin that clings to us and persevere in running the race that lies before us." Good advice at any time.

And the Gospel reading reminds you that Jesus did once very clearly say, "I have come to set the earth on fire, and how I wish it were already blazing."

Let's just stay with that one idea today. Let's linger on the wish that Jesus disclosed. Let's ponder the implications of the mission he expressed, namely, "I have come to set the earth on fire." He himself was fired up with enthusiasm; he was focused and purpose-driven.

He was speaking metaphorically, of course, when he said he came to light a fire on the earth. He had no scorched earth policy. He did not want to destroy the earth by fire. But he surely did want to "fire us up" with enthusiasm for his Gospel, to "ignite" our zeal for the spread of his Gospel and the salvation of our brothers and sisters in the human community. He wanted to spread a fire of love and concern for the poor in our world. He was something of a firebrand for justice and he surely wanted his followers to be enthusiasts for justice too.

He may even have thought of the faith that was his gift to us as something like a bed of embers that required fanning from time to time, fanning that raised the flame of faith to a higher intensity in prayer. I can't say for sure, and I don't want to dwell on that possibility now. I do, however, want to direct your attention to the fire-like enthusiasm Jesus had for the spread of the Gospel and invite you to think for a while now about where that enthusiasm is in your life and in your world. Indeed, I'd like you to think about the degree of intensity of your personal enthusiasm for the cause of Christianity in your world, for the spread of the word and way of life that Christ brought to our world. He chose to establish a Church as the vehicle for his mission. What is your enthusiasm for that Church today? And it is fair to ask, what is our Church's enthusiasm for the cause of Christ? That may sound strange, but we have to wonder if we are getting too comfortable, too detached from the urgent problems of hunger, poverty, and human need that were real concerns to the heart of Christ.

How fired-up are you and your Church today to continue the work Jesus began—preaching the good news to the poor, healing the sick, saving sinners, sanctifying all? Is the fire going out in Catholic education, Catholic healthcare, Catholic social services? Are there seats on governing boards of Catholic hospitals, schools, colleges, and service agencies waiting to be filled by people with your skills and resources, if only you were sufficiently enthusiastic to want to serve in this capacity? Are volunteer service opportunities failing to attract Catholic hands and hearts because Catholic ears no longer hear Jesus saying, "I have come to set earth on fire?"

Where is the fire today? Where are the Catholics who want to be priests for the parishes, nuns and brothers for the schools, nurses for the Catholic hospitals and assisted living communities, trained professionals for the Catholic social service agencies?

In an altogether different and quite secular setting, I remember when California Governor Ronald Reagan dismissed the first chancellor and twelfth president of the University of California, Clark Kerr. Kerr said he left the university just as he came into it—"fired with enthusiasm." Football coach Vince Lombardi was famous for saying "you've got to come to this team fired with enthusiasm or you're going to find yourself leaving this team fired with enthusiasm."

That message gets through to professional athletes; it has to start now getting through to contented Catholics who seem not to be noticing that the quality of Catholic service is declining and the level of commitment to Catholic institutions needs to be shored up with both professional and volunteer Catholic commitment.

You may have noticed that I avoided comment on those troubling lines in today's Gospel where you hear Jesus asking, "Do you think I have come to establish peace on the earth? No, I tell you, but rather division. From now on a household of five will be divided, three against two and two against three; a father will be divided against his son and a son against his father, a mother against her daughter and a daughter against her mother, a mother-in-law against her daughter-in-law and a daughter-in-law against her mother-in-law."

I'm really not sure what to make of that. There is an enigma associated with the mission of Jesus. It is fairly obvious—and he, of course, was well aware—that his ministry would bring discord. Go back to the second chapter in the Gospel of Luke (2:34) and you will find the wise old man Simeon saying to Mary, when she brought the infant Jesus into the temple, "Behold, this child is destined for the fall and rise of many in Israel, and to be a sign that will be contradicted."

Jesus was and still is a sign of contradiction. He is an enigma. He is also the Prince of Peace. Nonetheless, his teachings will be a source of division. That should not scandalize us. Neither should it prevent us from standing up and speaking up for all things Catholic, while dedicating our time, talent, and treasure to the advancement of Catholic institutions. We simply cannot permit the fire to go out!

Even recently, as for example, when the Vatican's Pontifical Council for Justice and Peace, headed by African Cardinal Peter Turkson, issued a document in October 2011 analyzing the moral failings of modern economic life, the recommendations were met with ridicule in some Catholic quarters and warm approval in others. That document, by the way, was titled: "Towards Reforming the International Financial and Monetary Systems in the Context of Global Public Authority." We'll save that for another day. Today, let's simply acknowledge that there is and probably always will be division in our Church. But it is our Church and we should let ourselves get fired up once again about sustaining its mission.

54

Twenty-First Sunday of the Year

The Two Wells

Isaiah 66:18–21; Psalm 117; Hebrews 12:5–7, 11–13; Luke 13:22–30

A reflective reading earlier this week of the selection you just heard from the Letter to the Hebrews prompts me to relate to you two stories, each involving a well—that's right, a well, the kind you draw water from or can accidentally fall into. But first, listen again to the reading from Hebrews:

> You have forgotten the exhortation addressed to you as sons: "My son [and we would add, "my daughter"] do not disdain the discipline of the Lord or lose heart when reproved by him; for whom the Lord loves, he disciplines; he scourges every son [or daughter] he acknowledges." Endure your trials as "discipline"; God treats you as sons [his own]. For what "son" [or daughter] is there whom his father does not discipline?... At the time, all discipline seems a cause not for joy but for pain, yet later it brings the peaceful fruit of righteousness to those who are trained by it. So strengthen your drooping hands and your weak knees. Make straight paths for your feet, that what is lame may not be disjointed but healed. (Heb 12:5–7, 11–13)

There is an old story called, "Shake It Off," about a farmer faced with the problem of trying to extricate his donkey from a deep well. The well was dry, just about useless, and somehow or other the donkey fell into it. For hours the farmer tried to rescue the screeching and crying donkey. Admitting defeat in this effort, the farmer decided that the donkey was doomed and the well wasn't of any use either, so he called several neighbors and asked them to help in the task of shoveling dirt to bury the donkey and seal off the well.

When the shovels full of dirt first fell on the donkey it squealed and stomped, but the farmer and his friends kept on shoveling. In a few moments there was quiet and the shoveling continued. Moments later the farmer looked down into the well and saw an interesting sight. As each shovelful of dirt fell on his back, the donkey shook it off and took a step up. The shake-off and step-up survival strategy continued until the donkey reached the surface, hopped out of the well and trotted away.

And the moral of the story is, of course, that life will shovel dirt on you from time to time. How will you react? The story suggests that you can shake it off and step up; your troubles can become stepping-stones

As I said, I thought of that story when I read the words from Hebrews: "Do not disdain the discipline of the Lord or lose heart when reproved by him." Not an exact parallel here, of course, between discipline flowing from the Lord's love and shovels full of dirt falling as the result of a farmer's frustration. But at the time the trials or discipline are being endured, love is not obvious and, as Hebrews puts it, it "seems a cause not for joy but for pain, yet later it brings the peaceful fruit of righteousness to those who are trained by it."

Each of us needs that training, and, like it or not, we receive from time to time opportunities to benefit from trials and various setbacks if not inflicted on us by the Lord, at least permitted by the Lord who loves us. Often, however, it is difficult to see through the pain to the faithful, reliable, dependable, unfailing love of God standing there behind it all.

In the Style section of *The Washington Post* some years ago (August 19, 2001), there was a page-one story under the headline, "Up in Smoke" that continued on the back page under a second headline: "Out of the Ashes: Loss, Despair, More Hard Work." It was a report of how three small Falls Church, Virginia businesses burned and how their owners had to decide, in the *The Post's* words, to "Start another chapter or finish the book." One of the three businesses that went up in flames in a two-story warehouse fire was Quinn's Auction House owned by my Holy Trinity parishioners Paul and Cathy Quinn and their son David. In the words of *The Post* reporter, a day or two after the fire, "Rain had fallen steadily since dawn, and by mid-afternoon everything droops but Paul Quinn's attitude. 'Through fire and flood we go on,' he says.... 'I have worked with enough families in distress to appreciate what I still have.... There are a whole lot of things in life that could be worse than what we're going through.'" Not everyone is a strong as Paul Quinn, and his wife Cathy, and their son David. Their faith enables them to "shake it off and take a step up!"

Remarkably, even perversely, we sometimes interpret our trials as sure signs of our worthlessness, our unworthiness. We don't emerge from the trials as better persons; we emerge with a darker perception of ourselves, a growing conviction of our own inadequacy and worth-lessness. That problem can be addressed by my second well story.

This one begins in a situation in which you may recall being once yourself, as a young child. Did you ever, when you were about five years old, stand by the bathroom sink and watch your father shave? That's where this story starts.

A youngster standing there watching his father shave, asked his dad, "Where does God live?" And without missing a swipe of the razor, the father answered, "In a well." Minutes later, when the clean-shaven father arrived at the breakfast table, his wife looked at him quizzically and asked "What's all this you're telling him about God living in a well?" Then the dad realized that he had practically been talking in his sleep and the answer he gave came from a thirty-year-old memory of an encounter he had on a summer morning in front of his childhood home in Poland. Along the dirt road in front of his farmhouse came a small band of Gypsy giants—five or six swarthy, bearded fellows whose size and swagger held him spellbound. One of these men went over to the well, pulled up the bucket, held it as if it were a coffee cup and took a deep drink. He unfurled his colorful neckerchief and dried off his beard and eyed the boy. "Where does God live?" he asked the youngster. He then looked over the edge into the well as the fascinated child walked up closer to him. The Gypsy then turned and lifted the youngster, spun him around, and held him face down so that he could look directly into the well and the mirror-like surface of the water. "What do you see down there?" he asked, and the boy said, "I don't see anything but myself." Then spinning the boy back and dropping the youngster's feet to the ground, the Gypsy said: "And now you know where God lives!"

So many of us become so easily convinced of our unworthiness, we forget that our faces mirror the God who dwells within. You may think it is a not-so-good-looking face, a too-fat face, a face too old or too low or high above the ground, but that's the face that God chooses to live behind.

You may have been disciplined too harshly, unfairly, and severely; your experience of "father" may have been so negative that you unconsciously have transferred all that negativity to your perception of God as father. "For what 'son' is there whom his father does not discipline?" asks the Letter to the Hebrews. Sure, you may have had a few run-ins with your father. You may even feel put upon by God because of events or circumstances in your life. But don't fall into the trap of letting your mind twist your picture of God into an angry umpire just waiting to call you "out" at the plate, instead of picturing him as he really is, a loving father waiting—like the father of the Prodigal Son— to welcome you home. Why? Because he loves you, you who are made forever lovable by the divine life there within!

So, shake it off, and step up.

And never forget where God lives—no, not in a well, but in you!

55

Twenty-Second Sunday of the Year

Conduct Your Affairs with Humility

Sirach 3:17–18, 20, 28–29; Psalm 68; Hebrews 12:18–19, 22–24a;
Luke 14:1, 7–14

I had a friend in college who had a party routine where, with mock sincerity, he would give a speech on humility and declare to all just how humble he was. "Humility is essential for success," he would say. "If you can fake that, you've got it made." And then he would protest that he wanted to be serious for a moment and offer his definition of humility, which was: "Humility is knowing your place and keeping it." And he would add a throwaway line, "Can I help it, if my proper place is at the top?"

He became a lawyer and capped his career with a seat on the Supreme Court of the Commonwealth of Pennsylvania.

Well, Sirach speaks to you this morning about humility. The Book of Sirach offers you a wonderful exposure to Israelite wisdom literature. It is gentle wisdom that you heard today in the first reading: "My child, conduct your affairs with humility, and you will be loved more than a giver of gifts." Now there's a congenial quid-pro-quo. Be humble and you will be loved, not only show yourself to be lovable, but be, in fact, loved.

"Humble yourself the more, the greater you are," says Sirach, "and you will find mercy in the sight of God." You're familiar with the saying, "The bigger they are, the harder they fall," but not all "big" shots pay much attention to that dictum. The wisdom you heard proclaimed this morning says, in effect, the bigger you are the more attentive you should be to humility. "The mind of the wise," says Sirach, "appreciates proverbs, and the ear that listens to wisdom rejoices." Are you wise enough to listen or, in your case, are the ears largely ornamental?

Listen you must today to Jesus, as Luke presents him in this morning's Gospel. Jesus is the embodiment of wisdom and what he says here in Luke's Gospel is an extension and refinement of the Israelite wisdom that Sirach proclaimed.

Luke locates Jesus in the home of a big shot, "one of the leading Pharisees." And noticing the way the invited guests were scrambling for the best places at table, Jesus told a parable, a story that gently and wisely makes the point. Don't grab the place of honor, he counsels, because chances are someone with a bit more heft than you have will arrive and you'll be asked to step down. No, take the "lowest place," the bottom rung, and you can expect your host to come to you and invite you to move up "to a higher position."

Rank is part of reality, but holding back or standing down is part of humility.

All this by way of preparation for the parable's central point: "For everyone who exalts himself will be humbled, but the one who humbles himself will be exalted." Think about that. Jesus, in his very practical wisdom, appeals to your proper and enlightened self-interest. He doesn't say, "Be a doormat and I will nail you down to hold you securely in place—at the bottom." No, he's saying, in effect, "Put the other fellow first, hold back, step aside, yield the spotlight—and trust me. You'll be okay. I guarantee it."

Some of you may have followed the great bicycle race in 2001—the Tour de France—and noticed that Lance Armstrong, already famous as a past winner and victor over cancer, was in the lead when his closest competitor had an accident, taking a tumble off the road and down an embankment, losing dignity, but hurting neither himself nor his bike. He did lose precious time, but he pulled himself together and scrambled back into the pack of racers. Armstrong slowed down enabling this closest rival to catch up to where he would have been without the spill, and then Armstrong let it all out to move farther ahead and win the race. "The one who humbles himself will be exalted." You can count on it.

You may be skeptical. Can you really count on moving up? Regaining the lead? Recapturing self-esteem? Well if you can't count on this Gospel principle of yielding to others and being better off because of that, what can you count on? Lean and mean? Get no mercy; give no mercy? Dog eat dog? Cutthroat competition? Me first?

Remember, the winner in a rat race is still a rat!

Our challenge, as we reflect on this ancient wisdom, is not to try to figure out how we can follow Christ in open sandals on dusty roads; our challenge is to figure out how we can follow Christ on downtown sidewalks and in glitzy skyscrapers where humility is all too often in dangerously short supply. The shortage is dangerous because our future as humans depends on our ability to live together humanly. You can't be truly human without being considerate, compassionate, and kind. The human community won't function well and hold together unless more of us take to heart the maxim that he or she who embraces humility will wind up being appropriately exalted.

Now that your ear is indeed "attentive" to this portion of ancient wisdom, keep on listening. "Then he [Jesus] said to the host who invited him, 'When you hold a lunch or a dinner, do not invite your friends or your brothers or your relatives or your wealthy neighbors, in case they may invite you back and you have repayment. Rather, when you hold a banquet, invite the poor, the crippled, the lame, the blind; blessed indeed will you be because of their inability to repay you. For you will be repaid at the resurrection of the righteous.'"

This is not a Scripture passage intended to put catering companies out of business. In our big cities where power lunches and black-tie dinners prevail, it seems quaint to say, "When you hold a lunch or a dinner, do not invite your friends or your brothers or your relatives or your wealthy neighbors, in case they may invite you back and you have repayment." Repayment may be just what you need to conduct business, to do the good you want to do. And just try never inviting friends or relatives to your home and see where that gets you. What's that going to mean for family solidarity, let alone Christian charity? Certainly, you have to invite them, but invite them for the right reasons, not selfish reasons; do it for their good, not for your own.

Dropping a dollar in a beggar's hand helps, but it falls short of what is being called for here. Inviting unattractive people to your party is praiseworthy, but still short of the ideal being proposed here. Filling up your invitation list with persons below your own socioeconomic status shows good will and is often enough to incur the wrath of a spouse who may not be moved, as you are, by the power of this Gospel. I know of one exasperated wife who complained about her good-hearted and well-known husband to a friend, "I don't know anyone who has such a propensity for downward social mobility," she said.

We all try to be upwardly mobile. We all catch ourselves at times looking past the "less important" person who has you engaged in conversation in order to see where the "really important" people are in the room. And we can laugh about it, and reflect on our own insecurities, our worldly ambitions, and our vulnerabilities, as we pray: "Lord, we are social climbers who give you thanks for bringing us to our knees in a prayer for humility. We know we need it. We know it won't hurt. And we know we'll be contributing to a better world whenever we get a little closer to the poor, the crippled, and the lame, and become more concerned with meeting the needs of others than having our own needs met by them. And we make this prayer in the name of our friend Jesus who tells us today, 'For everyone who exalts himself will be humbled, but the one who humbles himself will be exalted.' May we have the wisdom to make those words our own."

Amen.

56

Twenty-Third Sunday of the Year

Renunciation and Discipleship

Wisdom 5:13–18; Psalm 90; Philemon 9:10, 12–17; Luke 14:25–33

Today's Gospel message is direct, sobering, and even a bit frightening. "Everyone of you who does not renounce all his possessions," says Jesus, "cannot be my disciple."

But his message is even more demanding than that. The Gospel reading opens with Jesus having a great crowd following him and he turned to them and said: "If any one comes to me without hating his father and mother, wife and children, brothers and sisters, and even his own life, he cannot be my disciple."

What? Separating yourself (that's what "hating" means in this context) from parents, spouse, children, brothers and sisters, even from your very self as a precondition for following Christ? That doesn't seem to make a whole lot of sense. Indeed it flies in the face of the loves and loyalties we are expected to have, the commitments we are expected to keep, the commitments we are bound to keep by virtue of promises made and our state in life.

And notice that Jesus is not speaking only to single men and women here—the unattached, as we sometimes call them—the ones who in our day might answer a call to priesthood or religious life; no, he is speaking to all of us, married and single alike. But how are we to understand what he is saying? How can we resist the temptation simply to brush these words aside, dismissing them out of hand as not applicable to us, and then just going about our usual business? That's not an option. We have to be attentive to his words. We meet him there in the Gospel; you cannot simply tell him this doesn't apply to you. It does apply, but how?

Let me speak to you today about renunciation and discipleship. The Gospel urges us to travel light, to get by with just the essentials. There is something freeing in that, and the Gospel, after all, is really about freedom. The truth will make you free, Jesus said. Your faith will free you, he promised. So let's exercise our freedom in the face of these Gospel lessons to say something about renunciation (and the freedom it brings) and discipleship (which is the vocation each one of us has).

"Whoever does not carry his own cross and come after me," says Jesus to you today, "cannot be my disciple." Well, surely, you want to be his disciple, so you have to confront the cross, look it in the eye, shoulder it and be on your way on the path of discipleship. The cross here is a metaphor for duty, sacrifice, self-denial, service to others; the cross is a way of talking about life's challenges at any age and life's limits as the elder years set in. Illness is a cross. Retirement can be a cross. Loneliness can be a cross for many. There is much more than voluntary self-denial associated with the cross. There is risk (I'm not speaking of rash recklessness) as well as worry for those of you who are young along with a lot of hard work ahead of you. There is defeat and failure at times and frequent discouragement along the way. There is what you might call just the inescapable burden of living. All of this can be viewed as a cross to carry. And the short-term goal, as you know from what happened to Jesus on Calvary, is not an attractive one, although it is through the cross that you move to victory, just as through death you move on to eternal life.

You need courage. Jesus knows this as he invites you to take up your cross and follow him. He may have inspired Hemingway to write that courage (Hemingway called it "guts") is "grace under pressure." Jesus will supply the grace. Life will impose the pressure. You have to be free enough to live bravely; hence the need for renunciation in your life.

We Christians are invited to live an ethic of renunciation. We have to say no to ourselves. We have to distance ourselves from things and, at times, from others whom we are called upon to love. Hence Jesus can speak of "hating" your parents, spouse, children, friends—not in a sense of rejecting them, certainly not in a sense of harming them or neglecting them, just not permitting them (and your love for them) to come between you and Jesus. Does that sound strange? Not if you take it to mean that you and they should be going to Jesus together. Your journey to and with them is bound up with your journey to him.

Similarly with your possessions. You have to renounce them in the sense of not permitting yourself to be possessed by your possessions. That kind of possession can happen without your even being aware of it. Materialism and consumerism are viruses that abound in contemporary society. They can attack you at any time. You've got to immunize yourself against being possessed by your possessions by taking large doses of the Gospel message. One such message is up for your consideration today. It is a message of renunciation and discipleship.

Along with what I've already quoted from today's Gospel message, you can hear Jesus say: If one of you who decides "to construct a tower does not first sit down and calculate the cost to see if there is enough for its completion," you're looking at trouble. And that's a fair observation. It too has something to say about discipleship. You don't want to begin and not follow through. You don't want to start out and not complete the journey. You don't want to begin without having sufficient resources to make that discipleship solid and enduring. Have your eyes wide open. Know what you are getting into.

Similarly, Jesus suggests that you put yourself in the shoes of one going into war—"a king marching into battle, would [he] not first sit down and decide whether with ten thousand troops he can successfully oppose another king advancing upon him with twenty thousand troops?" The arithmetic is simple and compelling. But first you have to do the calculation! You have to have the facts; you have to plan; you have to be strategic. And in this all-important matter of discipleship the strategy is not complicated. You have to unburden yourself of the hold your possessions might have on you. You cannot be tied down with attachments. You have to be free to move, to move wherever Christ, who is always on the move, might be calling you.

That's what disciples do and all of you are called to discipleship!

57

Twenty-Fourth Sunday of the Year

"Christ Jesus Came into the World to Save Sinners"

Exodus 32:7–11, 13–14; Psalm 51; 1 Timothy 1:12–17; Luke 15:1–32

(*Note*: This homily was originally delivered shortly after the terrorist attacks of September 11, 2001 on the World Trade Towers and the Pentagon.)

"This saying is trustworthy," writes Paul to Timothy in the words you heard in the second reading today, "and deserves full acceptance: Christ Jesus came into the world to save sinners." That's the meaning of the name Jesus—"Yahweh saves." That's who Jesus is. "Christ Jesus came into the world to save sinners."

On September 15th, we celebrate throughout the Catholic world the feast of the Triumph of the Cross—the Exaltation of the Cross. And in the morning prayer of the Church on that great day of remembrance, the praying Church worldwide repeats in antiphonal praise these words: "To destroy the power of hell Christ died upon the cross, clothed in strength and glory, he triumphed over death."

He triumphed over death. He came into the world to save sinners. He died upon the cross to destroy the power of hell.

On September 11, 2001, dear friends, we witnessed evil in our world. We looked into the darkness of the dehumanized heart. We caught a glimpse of the power of hell. We lost—some of us—friends, family, loved ones, if only for a while as our faith assures us, but they are, nonetheless, lost to life on this earth. All of us have lost many we did not know but with whom we shared citizenship in this "land of the free and home of the brave." We lost others with whom we shared not citizenship but brotherhood and sisterhood in the human community, others with whom we were locked—hand in hand—in our shared human nature.

We pray for the victims whose unimaginable suffering we still struggle to comprehend by way of remembrance. We pray for the perpetrators whose evil actions we cannot imagine but struggle now to forgive.

"This saying is trustworthy and deserves full acceptance: Christ Jesus came into the world to save sinners." All of us are sinners who accept, and are accepted by, Christ Jesus. He died upon the cross "to destroy the power of hell," and standing with him, as we do today, we are not powerless in the face of the evil that we encounter in our world.

We are a people of hope. We hope not in a vague and undefined future; we hope in a merciful, all-powerful God. If God is all-powerful, we might be asking ourselves, why did he not prevent 9/11 from happening, why did he stand by as thousands suffered and died? For the same reason, I must tell you, that God stood by and permitted his Son to die on the cross for our salvation.

God permits evil, but does not positively will it to happen. God's permissive will opens the door to the abuse of human freedom, to human beings using their own free will (that which makes them human) to do evil things. God will not suppress human freedom, just as God will not suspend the law of gravity or other physical laws of nature. If you freely choose to act against those laws, as unfathomable as that choice may be, you live or die with the physical consequences of that choice. But God is always there to rescue you from the moral consequences of your evil, sinful choice, if you simply turn to him and seek his mercy. Mercy is God's ever available and always effective act of rescue. May God have mercy on them all—victims and criminals—whose deaths brought so many of us to our knees in prayer.

Today's Gospel reading, from the 15th chapter of Luke, is a celebration of mercy. Yes, a celebration. "Rejoice with me because I have found my lost sheep." "Rejoice with me because I have found the coin that I lost." "My son, you are here with me always; everything I have is yours. But now we must celebrate and rejoice, because your brother was dead and has come to life again; he was lost and has been found."

Rejoice in your faith today, dear friends. Rejoice in your hope—hope in a saving God who has and will save you from your grief, your weakness, your powerlessness, your sin and sinfulness. Rejoice in the acceptance of the fact that "Christ Jesus came into the world to save sinners." That means you. That means all who lost their lives in the hijacked planes, in the buildings they struck, and in the rescue efforts that ensued on September 11, 2001.

Rejoice in your firm belief that mercy is God's always available and eternally effective act of rescue no matter how great the dimensions of your personal or national disaster.

A few days after the September 11 tragedy, a friend sent me an e-mail message that ended with this quotation from Gandhi: "When I despair, I remember that all through history the ways of truth and love have always won. There have been tyrants, and murderers, and for a time they can seem invincible, but in the end they always fall. Think of it...always."

58

Twenty-Fifth Sunday of the Year

Lift up Your Hands and Pray

Amos 8:4–7; Psalm 113; 1 Timothy 2:1–8; Luke 16:1–13

I recall preaching these Scripture texts while the memory of the nation was still reeling with images of the destruction of September 11, 2001. Our hearts were heavy with sorrow for the dead and pity for those they left behind. Our eyes remained fixed with admiring gratitude on the rescuers. One eyewitness described firefighters in the Trade Towers as, "running up an idle escalator that turned out to be their stairway to heaven." Our minds were apprehensive over what might happen next. Our hope was anchored in the Lord to whom we entrusted ourselves and our unknown future. Our love went out to all, including our enemies. And our hands were willing to help in whatever way we could.

The mind of St. Paul, expressed in the Letter to Timothy, spoke directly to each one of us then and again today. It is uncanny that these words were in a text already in print and scheduled to be proclaimed everywhere in the Catholic world just days after the terrorist attacks: "It is my wish, then, that in every place the [people] should pray, lifting up holy hands, without anger or argument" (1 Tim 2:8).

Emotions ran high then and now; we cannot deny them. Anger still lurks within, but it can be controlled. Arguments have ensued and will indeed rage, but we pray that rage will not displace reason, that hatred will not fill a vacuum created by absentee love.

"It is my wish, then, that in every place the [people] should pray, lifting up holy hands, without anger or argument."

The prayer of the community, according to Paul's instruction, should not be marred by internal dissention.

For what then shall we pray today, dear friends? For peace, for justice, for security, for safety, for healing, for unity. For those who have died, for their families and dear ones, for those who were rescued, for their rescuers. For the caregivers. For those who are unemployed in the wake of economic disruption. For professional defenders of public order and safety, for strategists, diplomats, elected and appointed government officials. For all who stand in harm's way.

"It is my wish, then, that in every place the [people] should pray, lifting up holy hands, without anger or argument."

For whom else shall we pray? For ourselves, of course, that our hands may indeed be "holy," and that our arguments may be holy too, and "without anger," without hate. We should pray too for interfaith and intercultural understanding, for an end to bigotry, fanaticism, and hatred. Listen again to the opening of the selection from First Timothy that was proclaimed as our second reading today: "Beloved: First of all, then, I ask that supplications, prayers, petitions, and thanksgivings be offered for everyone, for kings and for all in authority, that we may lead a quiet and tranquil life in all devotion and dignity. This is good and pleasing to God our savior, who wills everyone to be saved and to come to knowledge of the truth. For there is one God. There is also one mediator between God and the human race, Christ Jesus, himself human, who gave himself as ransom for all."

"For all..." We can never permit ourselves to forget that he "gave himself as ransom for all." We, therefore, pray for all.

But let me invite you to pause for a moment today and think only of yourself. If you feel guilty (they call it "survivor's guilt") because others died and you escaped their fate, if you feel guilty, let go of that guilt; it can only harm you. If you feel grateful that you were spared from injury or death in the September 11th disaster that took others just like you, perhaps others known to you, dear to you, if you are grateful, let it be gratitude with a purpose. Purposeful gratitude can set your course for the future. Life does and will go on; it goes on into a future that is hidden from our eyes but secure in the sheltering hands of God. Purposeful gratitude—on your way to an unknown future—let that be your disposition now. But how will that gratitude be shown?

I recall participating not long after 9/11 in a strategic planning meeting for a large and complex not-for-profit organization. Strategic planning always looks to the future. It begins with strategic thinking, and strategic thinking begins with the question, "What sets us apart?"

Four options were put on the table for consideration by the organization's decision makers and their advisers. Four options that any one of you might consider as applicable to yourself as you get on with life in the wake of a disaster in the immediate past and great uncertainties in the immediate future. Those four options were (for the organization) and are now (for you): (1) stay the course; (2) stay the course, but modify objectives; (3) modify objectives and realign organizational structure; (4) significantly modify strategy. Any one of these may be perfectly appropriate for you, and only you can make that judgment. Only you can choose your next steps propelled, as they will be, by purposeful gratitude.

What sets you apart? Your faith, your vocational commitments, your particular circumstances. How does that all look to you now looking back to September 11th? (A friend sent me an e-mail message immediately after 9/11 that read, "Someday your whole life is going to pass before your mind's eye in a flash, a split second, do what you can now to make sure that you're going to like what you see!") Given your faith-based disposition toward purposeful gratitude, gratitude with a purpose, what option is the right one for you? Stay the course? Stay the course, but modify objectives? Modify objectives and realign your structure (in the sense of realigning your values or altering the way you typically and routinely do things? Significantly modify strategy? The choice is yours.

This is the kind of thinking that you have to bring to prayer as you lift up your hands without anger or argument. Our parish retreat program can assist you with this. Or, you can do it on your own in the setting of reflection, Scripture reading, Eucharist, the sacrament of reconciliation, or with help from others in spiritual direction and spiritual conversation. You ought to be talking to yourself about your options and talking to others whom you trust and who love you. At the end of World War II which, as you know, came to an abrupt end made possible by the use of atomic power against living humans, James Agee wrote these powerful and prophetic words for *Time* magazine:

In an instant, without warning, the present had become the unthinkable future. Was there hope in that future, and if so, where did hope lie?....

When the bomb split open the universe and revealed the prospect of the infinitely extraordinary, it also revealed the oldest, simplest, commonest, most neglected and most important of facts: that each man is eternally and above all else responsible for his own soul, and, in the terrible words of the Psalmist, that no man may deliver his brother, nor make agreement unto God for him.

Man's future has forever been shaped between the hands of reason and spirit, now in collaboration, again I conflict. Now reason and spirit meet on final ground, If either or anything is to survive, they must find a way to create an indissoluble partnership.

Now, after the hijacked airplanes split open the Trade Towers and the Pentagon, you, personally and individually, have to think about staying your course, or modifying your objectives, or realigning your values, or, perhaps, significantly modifying your strategy—whatever you decide is appropriate. No one but you can "make agreement unto God" for you. Collectively and as a faith community, we have to think about helping one another, and following St. Paul's advice that "in every place," including this Parish Community, "the [people] should pray, lifting up holy hands, without anger or argument."

September 11, 2001 has etched itself indelibly into history; we can never go back. But we can and will go forward, and dear Lord, we're counting on you to show us the way.

59

Twenty-Sixth Sunday of the Year

The Rich Man and Lazarus

Amos 6:1a, 4–7; Psalm 146; 1 Timothy 6:11–16; Luke 16:19–31

"Woe to those who are complacent," says the prophet Amos in this morning's first reading, and as we hear those words, our ears perk up. "But you, man of God," writes Paul in his first Letter to Timothy (our second reading today), "...pursue righteousness, devotion, faith, love, patience, and gentleness." And as we hear the recital of this list we check our personal spiritual shelves to see if an adequate supply of these items can be found there.

And then comes the excerpt from the Gospel of Luke, the story of Dives and Lazarus, the rich man and the poor man, a story of comfortable complacency on the side of Dives, the rich man, and the absence there of "righteousness, devotion, faith, love, patience, and gentleness." In their place we see purple garments, fine linen, and sumptuous dining in self-enclosed insensitivity.

"[L]ying at [the rich man's] door was a poor man names Lazarus, covered with sores, who would gladly have eaten his fill of the scraps that fell from the rich man's table."

One of the great jazz pianists of the 20th century was Mary Lou Williams. She had a mid-life spiritual conversion in response to personal and career problems in the 1950s. With pastoral assistance from Jesuit Fr. Tony Wood in New York City, Mary Lou became a Catholic. She resumed her interrupted career and came to see in the jazz music she played a form of resurrection theology. Through death to life, that's the meaning of resurrection theology for all believers. Through the dirge-like tempo of "Just a Closer Walk with Thee," the jazz musician could make music and spirits rise.

Some years later, through intermediary work by another Jesuit, Fr. Vincent O'Keefe, who was working in the Jesuit headquarters in Rome,

Mary Lou Williams was commissioned to compose a Mass in the jazz idiom by the Vatican's Pontifical Commission on Justice and Peace. She called it "A Mass for Justice and Peace." It was later choreographed and performed on Broadway as "Mary Lou's Mass" by the Alvin Ailey Dance Theater Group. All the elements of a Mass were included—the Gloria, the Lord's Prayer—all the parts with which you are familiar were danced out before your eyes and sung to great jazz music. For the Gospel in that Mass, Mary Lou chose the story you just heard, the story of the rich man and the poor man, of Dives and Lazarus.

A Mass for Justice and Peace. The Gospel of Dives and Lazarus. Think about the connection. I can still see the Alvin Ailey Group's dramatic dance rendition of the poor man rising from his misery and confronting the rich man in his complacency. I can still feel the intensity of the staged confrontation. And as I consider this Gospel today and frame it in the context of justice and peace; and as I think, as all of you cannot help but think in however confused a fashion, of the uncertainties and inequalities in a terrified world touched unjustly by terrorism, I think of the promise we have that we will possess a kingdom of love, justice, and peace.

We pray for peace. We pray for justice. We give and receive love as best we can. We pray "Thy kingdom come" in every Mass. The kingdom is coming. We can count on that. The reign of God, the dominion of God's will over all, is coming. We can't build the kingdom, we can only lower the barriers that hinder its coming. The kingdom is God's to give when the time is right. When will that be?

Recall the words of Jesus, recorded for you at the beginning of the Gospel of Mark (1:15): "This is the time of fulfillment," Jesus said, "The kingdom of God is at hand. Repent, and believe in the gospel." Why has the kingdom been at hand now for 2,000 years but not yet grasped? Why is the fulfillment of love, justice, and peace not yet in our midst? Because we have refused to "repent," to change our hearts, to accept the attitudinal turnaround that is required of anyone who hears and really believes the Gospel.

Millions have not yet heard the Gospel in any meaningful way. Millions who have heard and accepted the Gospel have not yet let it turn them around in a true north direction toward love, justice, and peace.

As this Gospel story tells you, the poor man died and "was carried away by angels to the bosom of Abraham." And the rich man died too and wound up in "the netherworld, where he was in torment." His plea for pity and a drop of water was denied. It was too late. The book was closed. "[B]etween us [namely Abraham and Lazarus] and you a great chasm is established" and you can't cross it. So the rich man pleaded that Lazarus be sent to warn the rich man's five surviving brothers "lest they too come to this place of torment." This drew another turndown from Abraham who added that if the living choose not to heed the teachings of Moses and the prophets, "neither will they be persuaded if someone should rise from the dead."

For us it is different. Someone did indeed rise from the dead. Jesus Christ, our Savior, faced death for our sake, passed through it for our salvation, made it possible for us to receive the gift of faith, and left behind for our consideration a Gospel of justice and peace. What do we make of that Gospel today? Indeed what do we make of today's Gospel, the story of the rich man and the poor man, in the light of the events of injustices in or world and the uncertainties that lie ahead?

We know that Afghanistan is one of the poorest countries in the world. We know that the Taliban are not Afghanistan, nor are they religious, nor are they following Islamic beliefs. We know that the Taliban represent a form of fascist tyranny that may quite justifiably have to be contained by force.

We know that knowledge always comes before love and that most of us have little or no knowledge of the other nations, cultures, and religions that are in the headlines in the wake of the terrorist attacks. We should therefore attend to the complacency that Amos warns us about. We have much to learn.

We know that the perpetrators must be apprehended. We know that increased security measures and intensified intelligence-gathering activity are fully justified, but we should heed Paul to Timothy as we map our strategies: "But you, man of God,...pursue righteousness, devotion, faith, love, patience, and gentleness."

The fact that we are surrounded by events is no indication at all that we will be overcome by events. We live under the banner of the cross. We have an interpretative framework within which to process the confusion, terror, and sorrow that have touched us where we live. We also have the Gospel calling us to love, justice, and peace, to lower, as I said, the human barriers that we permit to stand between us and the realization of justice, love, and peace in our lives, in our time. That kingdom is coming. We've got work to do. We've got to remove from ourselves and our human communities the roadblocks that our complacency permits to stand in the way of the coming reign of God.

And if you feel you need a bit of help in identifying and removing those roadblocks, think about making a retreat. Whatever you decide, with or without the help of a retreat and a retreat director, ponder these realities in prayer. Insert yourself into the scene that Luke's Gospel gives you today. Insert yourself between the rich man and the poor man and give some prayerful thought as to what you might be called upon by God to do now to close the gap.

60

Twenty-Seventh Sunday of the Year

"Increase Our Faith"

Habakkuk 1:2–3, 2:2–4a; Psalm 95; 2 Timothy 1:6–8, 13–14;
Luke 17:5–10

Today's readings raise three points that I, in turn, want now to raise for your consideration. Reflecting on these readings, I find one complaint, one request, and one image that I want to highlight for you now.

First, the image. In the second reading, the selection from Paul's second letter to Timothy, you heard these words: "...I remind you to stir into flame the gift of God that you have..." Think of your gift from God as the gift of faith. And imagine your faith to be like a bed of embers. The light, the heat, and the fire of faith are all there in the embers, but they are in a state of quiescence. They are subdued, unobtrusively present, just not immediately noticeable. Think of your faith, the gift of God, as a bed of embers. Then listen again to the instruction Timothy and those to whom he ministered received from Paul: "...I remind you to stir into flame the gift of God."

When you pray, you stir into flame the embers of faith. When you sing in liturgical song you pray as well and you are, of course, stirring into flame the embers of your faith. When you work day after day in the circumstances in which God's providence and your vocation have placed you, you are fanning into flame the embers of your faith. *"Laborare est orare,"* says the great Benedictine tradition of relatedness between work and prayer. And the tradition of Ignatian spirituality would say that you are capable of finding God in all things, if only you employ the optic of faith to see God in the ordinariness around you. Any believer, in any tradition of spirituality, is expected "to stir into flame the gift of God," the gift of faith, that is. Stir that bed of embers through prayer and you'll notice your prayer rising up to affect your lifestyle. That's what spirituality is—prayer elevated to a lifestyle. Let's move now from the image, the image of embers as portraying the gift of God, your faith, to point number two.

My second point is a complaint. You'll find it in the first reading, a selection from the Book of the prophet Habakkuk, who, speaking for all of us, raises a complaint that is particularly poignant for us today in these violent times: "How long, O Lord? I cry for help but you do not listen! I cry out to you, 'Violence!' but you do not intervene. Why do you let me see ruin; why must I look at misery? Destruction and violence are before me."

Prophetic words. Habakkuk then speaks for the Lord and offers to us the Lord's own answer: "See, the rash have no integrity; but the just one who is righteous, because of faith shall live." Hear the Lord say today, The just one, because of his or her faith shall live!

You and I, because of our faith, shall live through the sorrow and confusion of these days. Our brothers and sisters who lost their lives in the terrorist attacks on the Twin Towers and the Pentagon shall, because of their faith, also live; indeed they shall live forever. Let that be our consolation. Let that be our hope. And let that hope rise as a flame from the bed of embers that is your faith.

And my third point is a request, the request you heard the apostles make of Jesus in the segment of Luke's Gospel that was read just a few minutes ago: "And the apostles said to the Lord, 'Increase our faith.' The Lord replied, 'If you have faith the size of a mustard seed, you would say to [this] mulberry tree, 'Be uprooted and planted in the sea,' and it would obey you.'"

What are we to make of that? The comparison is striking. A mustard seed is tiny; a fully-grown mulberry tree is not easily uprooted and not likely to fly anywhere. Jesus does, as you must surely have noticed, employ hyperbole from time to time. He does so to make an instructional point, of course. And the point is that your desire for faith must be genuine; if it is true desire it will stretch your capacity to receive more of the gift of faith.

Jesus is God and God, as you know, does not ordinarily suspend the laws of nature, even if such suspension would save us from the ravages of tornadoes, floods, earthquakes, or hurricanes. He doesn't suspend the law of gravity to protect you from an accidental fall. He did not, as we are so painfully aware, suppress the free will of deranged humans who abandoned their humanity for terrorism and fanaticism, to murder thousands of innocent people, some known to some of us, all loved now by all of us who embrace them with the embrace of faith.

We say, "Increase our faith." That means broaden and deepen that bed of embers that is God's gift to us. And he says, in effect, "Fan that bed of embers." "Stir into flame the gift of God that you have." That rising flame will lift your spirit, heighten your courage, set you up to deal with the mulberry trees that you seem to be bumping into these days at every turn when it is so difficult to separate the forest of your fear and confusion from the trees of a daily life that must go on, and will indeed go on, because God wills it so.

The permissive will of God allows dreadful things to happen in our midst. The positive will of God calls us always to move forward—in faith, in friendship, in love for one another, in service to one another, in recommitment, in forgiveness, in hope.

Thank God for the embers of faith that are yours. Fan them now with prayer that rises to God with this Eucharist we offer in remembrance of Jesus and all who have gone before us marked with the sign of faith.

61

Twenty-Eighth Sunday of the Year

Leprosy and Gratitude

2 Kings 5:14–17; Psalm 98; 2 Timothy 2:8–13; Luke 17:11–19

The word "leprosy" jumps out at you from these readings today. We can take heart from the story of Naaman, the leper, who, as the selection you heard from the 2 Kings relates it, "went down and plunged into the Jordan seven times, according to the word of the man of God. His flesh became again like the flesh of a little child, and he was clean." And Naaman, according to this biblical story, went gratefully back to the man of God, Elisha, and offered him a gift, a token of gratitude. Elisha refused the gift prompting Naaman to declare that he will henceforth offer his gifts of thanks to no "other god except to the Lord."

Think for a few moments with me today, dear friends, about leprosy and gratitude—your leprosy, your gratitude.

I speak metaphorically, of course, when I mention your leprosy. You, thank God, are not touched by the chronic infectious disease that has afflicted humanity in the poor parts of the world since time immemorial, and continues to afflict an estimated 1.2 million poor people today. You know the history of mutilation, rejection, and exclusion from society that are associated with this dread disease.

Even though you are untouched by the disease, you can relate to the exhilaration felt by Naaman when he was cured. You can appreciate his impulse to give thanks.

You can also imagine yourself among those ten lepers who met Jesus as he was entering a small village on his way to Jerusalem. You heard the familiar story again in today's Gospel reading. Let yourself drop back two millennia; put yourself in that small platoon of pitiable people who encountered Jesus. There you are standing "at a distance" and, along with the others, raising your voice and saying: "Jesus, Master! Have pity on us!"

Go ahead. Say those words today in prayer, "Jesus, Master! Have pity on me." Say them at Communion time, say those words directly to the Lord, conscious, as you are, of your need for healing—spiritual healing, along lines perhaps of forgiveness and reconciliation; or healing of a broken spirit, spiritual healing needed to overcome discouragement, confusion, sadness. Your spiritual leprosy may indeed stand in need of the healing of hope, the healing that only hope can bring, and the hope that can bring that healing can be found only in the Lord. Here you are, face-to-face with him in prayer today. Seize the moment as best you can.

Return now to the Gospel story. "And when he saw them, he said, 'Go show yourselves to the priests.' As they were going they were cleansed.'" As they were going—just their turning toward him, just their desire for cleansing, resulted in their cleansing. Some of you should perhaps be showing "yourselves to the priests" in the sacrament of reconciliation—disclosing yourself as you see yourself before God, and in your sacramental encounter with Jesus seeking and gaining forgiveness, finding a cure for your leprosy.

You've had that experience before. In baptism. In sacramental absolution. In the forgiveness—human and divine—that you received simply because you asked for it with a sincere heart. "As they were going they were cleansed. And one of them, realizing he had been healed, returned, glorifying God in a loud voice; and he fell at the feet of Jesus and thanked him." He thanked him. He thanked him. And that thanking him laid down the foundation for the living out of the rest of his life in gratitude.

Would you have been that one? Or would you have been one of those Jesus asked about when he said, "Where are the other nine? Has none but this foreigner returned to give thanks to God?"

Leprosy and gratitude. Put the two together in your heart today, dear friends. Reflect on their relatedness in your life. You are free of physical leprosy. Are you grateful? You are, or can become free of spiritual leprosy. Are you grateful?

I'm convinced that if you had to reduce the entire content of religion to just one word, if you had to encapsulate the essential meaning of religion in just one word, that one word would be gratitude. So ask yourself, are you a grateful person? Have you "returned to give thanks to God?" What do you see yourself doing here before the altar on Sunday if it is not giving thanks to God? Let your life be grounded in gratitude. Let your outlook be colored by gratitude.

And let the foundation of your moral life be gratitude. Remember the old American vernacular where "much obliged" was a way of saying thanks? When you say thanks to God you declare yourself to be "much obliged," to have a moral obligation to cultivate an attitude before God of praise and thanksgiving, and to reach gratefully out to others to share what you have, to share generously of yourself in compassion and care, to be for them and not just simply for yourself. Much obliged! Reflect on that familiar expression and let it guide you through the weeks ahead as you move, by God's good grace, to new and higher levels of hope.

So, go ahead and say it today, "Jesus, Master! Have pity on us!" And be ever grateful for the response he will surely make to your plea.

62

Twenty-Ninth Sunday of the Year

Pray Always Without Becoming Weary

Exodus 17:8–13; Psalm 121; 2 Timothy 3:14—4:2; Luke 18:1–8

Two stories come to mind to reinforce the point made here by Jesus in this morning's Gospel about praying persistently without losing heart. Luke put it this way: "Then he [Jesus] told them [his disciples] a parable about the necessity for them to pray always without becoming weary." He told them the story of the crusty old judge who respected neither God nor his fellow humans. But the judge encountered a widow who refused to be intimidated and pressed him for a "just decision" against her adversary. She kept pressing him "for a long time," according to Luke. And the unjust judge gives in. "Because this widow keeps bothering me," he says, "I shall deliver a just decision for her lest she finally come and strike me."

And Jesus tells his disciples to "Pay attention to what the dishonest judge says," and invites them to make a comparison with God: "Will not God then secure the rights of his chosen ones who call out to him day and night? Will he be slow to answer them?" Of course not; he will be prompt. As Jesus put it, "I tell you, he will see to it that justice is done for them speedily." And then Jesus ends this parable with a curious, throwaway question: "But when the Son of Man comes, will he find faith on earth?"

Will he find the kind of faith that, as he told us before, can move mountains? Will he find persistence like that of the widow? The answer depends on you—on your faith, on your persistence in prayer, on your willingness to "pray always without becoming weary."

The first of the two stories that this Gospel passage brings to my mind occurred in New Orleans in the springtime of 1975. I was concluding my service as dean of arts and sciences at Loyola University there. At the prompting of the chair of the English Department, I made arrangements for the great novelist Walker Percy, who lived in Covington, Louisiana, across Lake Pontchartrain from New Orleans, to teach a course in writing at Loyola the following fall. Walker Percy agreed to take about a dozen students in a writing seminar and the condition of entry was submission of a writing sample for his inspection. Percy would read the samples and select his class based on their writing potential.

The local newspapers, the *New Orleans Times-Picayune* and *States-Item*, ran stories about this upcoming literary happening—a celebrity author becoming a Loyola professor—so the wider community knew that a famous writer would be on the Loyola University campus for the fall semester.

Now fast-forward a few years to the publication of a novel titled *Confederacy of Dunces* by John Kennedy Toole. Walker Percy, in a foreword to that novel, wrote that "I was in my office at Loyola" when I began to receive phone calls from a woman, a widow who persisted in pressing upon him the outrageous proposition that he should read the unpublished manuscript of a novel written by her dead son. She just wouldn't let up. So he agreed to review the manuscript, confident, he noted, that he would be able to read a few pages and then, with a clear conscience, just set it aside. But no. He read it all the way through; read it again, and decided that this was a novel more than deserving of publication. John Kennedy Toole had committed suicide. Some think his failure to get the book into print contributed to his depression. But his mother just wouldn't give up.

On Walker Percy's recommendation, the Louisiana State University Press published the novel, something university presses rarely do—publish novels. The book received critical acclaim and a Pulitzer Prize awarded posthumously to the dead son of a persistent mother. You can almost hear Percy saying, along with the judge in this morning's parable, "Because this widow keeps bothering me I shall deliver a just decision for her lest she finally come and strike me."

Be a pest when you pray. That's quite all right. Take Jesus at his word and recognize the "necessity" "to pray always without becoming weary."

The second story involves two Jesuits: Fr. Walter Ciszek who spent many years as a prisoner in Russia, seven of them in solitary confinement, and Fr. Ed McCauley who taught physics for many years at Gonzaga High School in Washington, DC. Ed McCauley and Wally Ciszek were Jesuit seminarians together—classmates, close friends.

Walter Ciszek was born in Shenandoah, Pennsylvania in 1904 and he entered the Society of Jesus at Poughkeepsie, New York in 1928. As a seminarian he responded to a call from the General of the Jesuit Order for volunteers to prepare themselves for service in Russia once the ban on religious practice there was lifted—whenever that would be. He was ordained a priest in the Byzantine rite in Rome in 1937 and assigned to the Jesuit mission in Albertyn in Eastern Poland in 1938. After the Russians invaded eastern Poland and closed his mission, Walter Ciszek crossed into Russia undercover in 1940, posing as an auto mechanic, hoping to be able to offer priestly service to those who had been deported to lumber camps in the Ural Mountains. He was arrested in June 1941 as a "Vatican spy" and sent to Moscow's Lubianka prison and subsequently sentenced to fifteen years of hard labor. Transferred to prison camps in Siberia after World War II, he was presumed dead by his family and the Jesuit order, but not by his friend Ed McCauley who was persistent in trying to locate him. In 1955, Ed McCauley received an indication that a package he had sent to his friend was received. Fr. McCauley, based in Washington at Gonzaga High School, began to contact the State Department and the Department of Justice with repeated reminders that a Jesuit priest, an American citizen, was being held against his will by the Soviets. One day in October 1963, Ed McCauley received a telephone call from Attorney General Robert F. Kennedy who said, "Your friend is going to arrive at Idlewild Airport tomorrow night." Kennedy had arranged a prisoner swap and gained Fr. Ciszek's freedom in return for the release of two Soviet agents who were being held by the United States.

Because a good friend would not give up, Wally Ciszek came back home where he lived another twenty-one years giving lectures, retreats, spiritual direction, and writing books that have inspired thousands of people.

So reflect on these stories today and reflect on yourself. Put yourself in that circle of disciples to whom Jesus told his parable "about the necessity for them to pray always without becoming weary." And present yourself to Jesus today as an answer to the question he used to conclude this morning's Gospel message: "But when the Son of Man comes, will he find faith on earth?"

You bet he will, you can say. He will find it in you and in your persistent prayer.

63

Thirtieth Sunday of the Year

"Everyone Who Exalts Himself Will Be Humbled;
The One Who Humbles Himself Will Be Exalted"

Sirach 35:12–14, 16–18; Psalm 34; 2 Timothy 4:6–8; 16–18;
Luke 18:9–14

This familiar Gospel story provides me with the opportunity to introduce you to an unfamiliar, even strange-sounding word, "humbition." It is an amalgam of the words humility and ambition and is being bandied about in business circles these days—an unlikely place to find solid spiritual advice. More on that in a moment.

The Gospel story is familiar to you. Two men entered the temple to pray. Jesus tells the story and Luke, who records it, tells us that Jesus is speaking "those who were convinced of their own righteousness and despised everyone else." Only you can really say if this story is intended for you! In any case, here it is: "Two people went up to the temple area to pray; one was a Pharisee and the other was a tax collector. The Pharisee took up his position and spoke this prayer to himself, 'O God, I thank you that I am not like the rest of humanity—greedy, dishonest, adulterous—or even like this tax collector. I fast twice a week, and I pay tithes on my whole income.' But the tax collector stood off at a distance, and would not even raise his eyes to heaven but beat his breast and prayed, 'O God, be merciful to me a sinner.' I tell you, the latter went home justified, not the former." And then Jesus concludes this famous story with the memorable words, "For everyone who exalts himself will be humbled, and the one who humbles himself will be exalted."

To what extent do you tend toward "self-righteousness?" To what degree to you tend to "hold everyone else in contempt?" Only you can say. Fair to say, however, I suspect, that not all of us are perfectly clean on those scores. So it is worth taking a moment or two now to slip into the temple observing each of these men and seeing to what extent either is present in ourselves. It has been said of the truly and irreformably arrogant person that "here in this life he is Pharisee, hereafter he is damned." None of us, of course, wants that verdict to ever fall upon us. So we can profit from observing the tax collector.

I said I would like to offer the notion of "humbition" as an appropriate value for you to consider; it is a value I recommend to Christian men and women in the world of business who want to maintain a proper balance between their commitment to follow a leader who described himself as "meek and humble of heart," and their effort to succeed in business. In other words, I recommend this term, humbition, to those who want to balance their religious faith and their effort to imitate Christ with their professional, daily, secular pursuits and Monday-through-Friday responsibilities.

An amalgam of the words humility and ambition, humbition means Spirit-driven, purposeful, forward motion that is grounded in humility, linked to service, and propelled by a desire to devote one's workplace efforts to the greater glory of God.

Let me begin my explanation of humbition with reference to a secular setting completely unrelated to the context of faith or spirituality, namely, a back-office service company SEI Investments in Oak, Pennsylvania, where the word "humbition" is held up for praise and imitation. "At SEI, the most effective leaders exude a blend of humility and ambition—humbition—that relies on the power of persuasion rather than formal authority" [See William C. Taylor and Polly LaBarre, *Mavericks at Work: Why the Most Original Minds in Business Win* (New York: Harper Paperback, 2008, p. 240)]. This book, *Mavericks at Work*, is where I first encountered the word humbition.

Later, William Taylor, one of the co-authors of Mavericks at Work, authored a book titled *Practically Radical: Not-So-Crazy Ways to Transform Your Company, Shake Up Your Industry, and Challenge Yourself* (William Morrow, 2011). In it he mentioned the notion of humbition again. He credits Jane Harper, a thirty-year veteran of IBM, "who devoted her career to transforming how the once-famously top-down organization, founded by the larger-than-life Thomas Watson, approaches innovation, collaboration, and leadership...." Humbition,

Jane Harper explains, is the blend of humility and ambition that drives the most successful businesspeople—an antidote to the hubris that infects (and undoes) so many executives and entrepreneurs" (*Practically Radical*, p. 197).

Jane Harper, according to Taylor, says the term "humbition" was coined by researchers at Bell Labs in an effort to describe the personal attributes of the most effective scientists and engineers.

Where it originated is not all that important for our present purposes. I simply want to make the point that the Christian in business has to be grounded in humility and determined to achieve (but not at any price). The Christian sees humility as a way to imitate Christ, and achievement in secular pursuits as a way to give glory to God. Both—the imitation of Christ and giving glory to God—are within reach of all Christians in business. This is not doormat spirituality; this is practical business advice!

Just to provide a bit more background, here is an excerpt from the text of a "manifesto" written in 2002 for young IBMers by John Wolpert and a few other IBM managers, including Jane Harper. They wanted to encourage emerging leaders within IBM. It is titled "Staying Extreme: How to Make a Difference in Any IBM Environment:"

> Humbition is one part humility and one part ambition. We notice that by far the lion's share of world-changing luminaries are humble people. They focus on the work, not themselves. They seek success— they are ambitious—but they are humbled when it arrives. They know that much of that success was luck, timing, and a thousand factors out of their personal control. They feel lucky, not all-powerful. Oddly, the ones operating under a delusion that they are all-powerful are the ones who have yet to reach their potential.... [So] be ambitious. Be a leader. But do not belittle others in your pursuit of your ambition. Raise them up instead. The biggest leader is the one washing the feet of the others. (*Practically Radical*, pp. 197–198.)

The point I want to emphasize here is simply that humility, as demonstrated in the life of Christ, is a highly desirable leadership characteristic. This is not unrelated to what Jim Collins has called "fierce resolve"—see "Level 5 Leadership: The Triumph of Humility and Fierce Resolve," *Harvard Business Review*, July–August 2005, 136–146. Collins says, "The most powerfully transformative executives possess a paradoxical mixture of personal humility and professional will." "Our discovery," says Collins, speaking of a five-year research project on the nature of effective leadership, "is counterintuitive. Indeed, it is countercultural."

Cultures are defined by dominant values. The dominant values in contemporary business culture are competition, individualism, greed, power, and accumulation of wealth. The dominant values in Catholic Christianity are love, humility, collaboration, sacrifice, service, and care for the poor. How do we bridge the two worlds? How do we remain authentic Christians while succeeding in the world of business?

Or, ask yourself, how you would describe the dominant culture within which the Pharisee of our Gospel story today lived and worked? And how would you describe the culture within which the tax collector lived and worked? Apparently, they were influenced by different dominant values and that was evident in their demeanor and attitudes there in the temple.

Jesus invites us all to be countercultural, against the values that dominate in our secular culture. If we are going to follow him, we have to be different. Even the folks at IBM noticed that back in 2002 and caught the idea in that memorandum I quoted earlier: "Be a leader. But do not belittle others in your pursuit of your ambition. Raise them up instead. The biggest leader is the one washing the feet of the others." That notion of washing the feet of others comes, quite obviously, right out of the Gospel that Jesus gave us to shape our outlook, form our values, and lead us to eternal life.

Here again today, we have a lesson from that Gospel that each of us would do well to heed: "For everyone who exalts himself will be humbled, and the one who humbles himself will be exalted." Adopt the notion of humbition; it will help keep you on track. It is working now for others in the real world of business; no reason why it cannot work for you.

64

Thirty-First Sunday of the Year

"To Seek and Save What Was Lost"

Wisdom 11:22—12:2; Psalm 145; 2 Thessalonians 1:11—2:2;
Luke 19:1–10

Listen again to the first sentence from today's first reading, the selection from the Book of Wisdom: "Indeed, before the Lord, the whole universe is like a grain from a balance, or a drop of morning dew come down upon the earth." Talk about a mind-stretching concept! Talk about getting a bit of help to keep things in perspective! Size yourself up as you listen to those words once again: "Indeed, before the Lord, the whole universe [all lands, all seas, all the planets, all people, all of creation] is like a grain from a balance, or a drop of morning dew come down upon the earth." Picture yourself then, "before the Lord."

Pretty small, yes; but not at all insignificant. "For you love all things that are," the reading goes on to say, speaking of the Lord, "and [you] loathe nothing that you have made." It may become easier for you to understand the profound meaning of all this when we come momentarily to consider the story of Zacchaeus, that small but by no means insignificant fellow who shows up in today's Gospel story.

But for now, stay fixed, dear friends, in your mind's eye, "before the Lord." Compare yourself, as the Book of Wisdom invites the comparison, with "the whole universe." See yourself from the perspective of the all-powerful, eternal, Triune God. See yourself as God saw you before you or anyone or anything else was even created.

That's the perspective St. Ignatius of Loyola would have you take if you were making the "Contemplation on the Incarnation" as he outlined it for you in his little retreat manual known as the Book of the *Spiritual Exercises.* Ignatius would have the retreatant contemplate "how the Three Divine Persons look down upon the whole expanse or circuit of all the earth, filled with human beings." Ignatius is inviting you to look over the shoulder of the Triune God, so to speak, to look out from before the moment of creation, before it all began, back when there was nothing but God: Father, Son, and Holy Spirit, existing from all eternity, not yet creating, but knowing all that was to come. Contemplate "how the Three Divine Persons look down upon the whole expanse or circuit of all the earth, filled with human beings," says Ignatius. "Since they are all going down to hell," he continues in words reminiscent of Dante's *Inferno*, written two centuries before the time of Ignatius. "Since they are all going down to hell" sounds shockingly harsh to us, but Ignatius intended those words to mean that the Triune God saw humans misusing their freedom, breaking away from God, choosing to live in a way that is out of tune with God and would, indeed, result in eternal alienation from God. And so, Ignatius continues, "They [the Triune God] decree in Their eternity that the Second Person should become man [Christ our Lord] to save the human race."

And Ignatius directs the retreatant to imagine the entire sweep of the earth and to see swarms of diverse people: "Some are white, some black; some at peace, and some at war; some weeping, some laughing; some well, some sick; some coming into the world, some dying." He wants you to use your imagination in listening to what people are saying to one another. And then he wants you to hear "what the Divine Persons say, that is, 'Let us work the redemption of the human race.'" And so the meditation leads on to the Annunciation and the Incarnation—God's way of launching the great enterprise of salvation, of "working the redemption of the human race"—including your redemption!

Yes, indeed, as the Book of Wisdom says so well, "Before the Lord, the whole universe is like a grain from a balance, or a drop of morning dew come down upon the earth." Where do you fit into all that? You do have a place. No bigger, perhaps, than the place Zacchaeus had, but a place nonetheless! You were there in God's eye from all eternity. And then when the Second Person of the Blessed Trinity did become man to walk the earth and to "work the redemption of the human race," he searched you out as he did Zacchaeus. And he said to you, as he said to Zacchaeus, who, as we juxtapose these two texts, is the one up above on high, looking down from his perch in a tree. And the Second Person of the Blessed Trinity is no longer way up there looking down from all eternity; no, he is down here below, inhabiting our flesh, walking our earth, and he the God-man looks up and says, "Zacchaeus, come down quickly, for today I must stay at your house." And Jesus went on to say to this little, insignificant fellow, as he says to you, who are so much more than a grain from a balance or a drop of morning dew, "Today salvation has come to [your] house."

These are words that all of us should hear today and take to heart. But especially favored today are those who are being baptized and those being received into full communion with the Church.

All of us together should "come quickly" to Jesus at this hour, for "Today, salvation has come to [our] house."

65

Thirty-Second Sunday of the Year

"May Our Lord Jesus Christ...Encourage Your Hearts"

2 Maccabees 7:1–2, 9–14; Psalm 17; 2 Thessalonians 2:16—3:5;
Luke 20:27–38

Dear Friends in Christ, permit me to let the seven brothers from 2 Maccabees (the first reading) and the seven brothers in today's Gospel selection from Luke go their separate ways this morning. I'm just not up to an appropriate exegesis, much less a meaningful homily capable of moving minds and hearts on the basis of these two scriptural accounts. But I would like to invite you to reflect a bit more on some of the words in the second reading, the selection from Paul's Second Letter to the Thessalonians. There are some remarkable phrases there. Listen again to the opening sentence:

"Brothers and sisters: May our Lord Jesus Christ himself and God our Father, who has loved us and given us everlasting encouragement and good hope through his grace, encourage your hearts and strengthen them in every good deed and word."

"Everlasting encouragement." "Good hope through his grace." Great phrases and, if I may say so, a possible source of encouragement for all of us right now. We all need encouragement. Not just some of the time, but all the time.

You're not Thessalonians; you live in another city, in another country, at another time. But St. Paul can pray for you today as he prayed for the Thessalonians centuries ago, and we can use Paul's words to pray for each other: "May our Lord Jesus Christ...encourage your hearts." May he do so indeed!

The psalmist in the 27th Psalm uses words that I often repeat and would warmly recommend to each of you this morning: "Wait for the LORD, take courage; be stouthearted, wait for the LORD!" If you wait for the Lord, he will indeed act. Call on the Lord in any circumstance, any situation, and the Lord your God will respond. Maybe not right away, maybe not exactly as you would want him to act, but he will act because you are the constant object of his unfailing love. So while you're waiting, "take courage, be stouthearted."

Paul reminded the Thessalonians, as you may need to be reminded this morning, that God "has loved us and given us everlasting encouragement and good hope through his grace." Chesterton once said something to the effect that hope is no virtue at all unless things are really hopeless! So when you're down, when your well has run dry, let the virtue of hope kick in. And your hope, of course, is in God, the all-powerful, all-loving God who knows you by name and cannot be anything but faithful to you no matter how faithless or careless you may have shown yourself to be toward him.

"But the Lord is faithful," says Paul in this morning's second reading; "he will strengthen you and guard you from the evil one." He will indeed. Let me tell you a true story to give you a bit of encouragement, to encourage you to convince yourself that, as Paul says, that "the Lord is faithful," faithful to you.

I had a friend, a retired army nurse, named Lillian Brill. She retired at the rank of full colonel and lived in a cottage in Annapolis near the Naval Academy. She was a doctoral graduate of the nursing school at The Catholic University of America and often returned, while I was president there, for plays in the Hartke Theater or concerts in the School of Music. She called me one day and asked me come over to Annapolis to help her plan her funeral. She had Hodgkin's disease and knew that her time was growing short. She wanted to have the Mass in the Naval Academy Chapel where she worshipped regularly and she was very clear in stating that there was to be "no doom and gloom" associated with the ceremony. She asked me to bring the dean of the School of Music along to participate in the planning, because, she said, she loved the violin and wanted several of her favorite selections to be part of the funeral liturgy.

So over we went to Annapolis to see Lillian on a beautiful, sunny spring morning. She had just had her monthly blood transfusion and was feeling good. She repeated the "no doom and gloom" instruction and explained why she felt that way. "I've read the Bible often," she said, "and I've underlined all the promises that God has made to us in Scripture. And if God is God, he can't be anything but faithful to his promises."

Now there's an echo, dear friends, of Paul's words to the Thessalonians; make them your own. As St. Paul said to the Thessalonians, "But the Lord is faithful; he will strengthen you and guard you from the evil one."

Lillian Brill died two weeks later and we followed her instructions to a T. We also let her speak for herself in the homily by reminding those who gathered to say farewell that "if God is God, he cannot be anything but faithful to his promises."

"Wait for the LORD, take courage; be stouthearted, wait for the LORD!"

Brothers and sisters: "May our Lord Jesus Christ himself and God our Father, who has loved us and given us everlasting encouragement and good hope through his grace, encourage your hearts and strengthen them in every good deed and word."

The late, great French Jesuit Teilhard de Chardin wrote an encouraging letter to Leontine Zanta on May 20, 1924, at a time she needed some encouragement. If you find yourself in need of encouragement today, hear these words as if they were addressed to yourself. Take them to heart, so to speak, so that your heart may experience the encouragement God wants you to enjoy: "Let yourself be carried along by events, once they are too strong for you. You have a great influence on many minds you are in contact with. Do not worry if you find this form of activity somewhat sporadic or disconnected. It is not essential that we should completely and distinctly understand our life, for it to be good and worthwhile. Often a life is fruitful through a side of it that one might be inclined to think little of."

Think about that. And let me close with the sentence Paul used to end this segment we've been considering from his Second Letter to the Thessalonians: "May the Lord direct your hearts to the love of God and to the endurance of Christ." Surely, by God's grace, you can endure. And as the late Jesuit theologian Walter Burghardt would tell you, his good friend and fellow theologian John Courtney Murray would often say to him when things were not going well, "Have courage, Walter, it's far more important that intelligence!"

66

Thirty-Third Sunday of the Year

Work and Preparation

Malachi 3:19–20; Psalm 98; 2 Thessalonians 3:7–12; Luke 21:5–19

We are celebrating in this Mass the "Rite of Acceptance into the Order of Catechumens" and the "Rite of Welcome" for those preparing for reception into full communion with the Catholic Church. This points us toward the Easter Vigil and marks the beginning of formal preparation for those who will be baptized and for those already baptized, but not yet confirmed nor participants with us at the Communion Table of the Lord. You all have a lot of work to do between now and Easter. So as we welcome you and congratulate you, we also encourage you to take the work of preparation not only seriously, but joyfully in response to the Lord who has called you to take this step.

You have work to do. And I want to talk about work for a few moments this morning. I'm prompted by the words you heard in the second reading, the selection from the Second Letter of St. Paul to the Thessalonians. These words are frequently quoted, often for the wrong reason, but quoted nonetheless. The Thessalonians were instructed that "if anyone was unwilling to work, neither should that one eat." As I say, that instruction is often misapplied to condemn poor people who, through no fault of their own, cannot work. The Christian community in Thessalonica had become "disorderly," according to Paul's letter; the people were "not keeping busy but minding the business of others. Such people we instruct and urge in the Lord Jesus Christ to work quietly and to eat their own food."

No need to probe into the history or the sociological surroundings of this instruction to the Thessalonians. Let us today simply reflect on our willingness—the willingness of each one of us in this congregation—to work, and the need for those we welcome today to "work quietly" between now and Easter in meeting their preparation responsibilities.

I recall getting a call years ago from a retired business executive who had come from Detroit to Washington as a consultant to a federal agency. I had known him for some years and he called to ask me to have lunch with him to discuss an important matter. At lunch he told me, as he put it, "the story of his life" from the days when he, a German Jew, was imprisoned in a concentration camp, through his arrival after the Second World War, with the help of some of the Americans who liberated him, into the United States and on to American citizenship, a one-year certificate program in engineering, and later employment with several major corporations. Along the way he married a Catholic but had no noticeable interest in any religion. Citing his happy marriage, his wonderful son and daughter, his unusual success in business, and his friendship with Catholics whom he admired, he then said, "There, at all these positive turning points in my life, I can see now the hand of God. So I've decided I want to become a Catholic." Knowing him well and realizing that his post-retirement age put him a few decades apart from most others who would be in the preparation class with him, should he decide to move forward, I said, "This is not like joining a country club, my friend; some serious preparation will be required of you." "I'll do anything," he replied, "just point me in the right direction." He proved to be an eager participant in the program that you catechumens are beginning today, and was baptized, as you will be, at the Easter Vigil. He worked at it.

Have you ever noticed a few quiet references to "work" in the Mass we celebrate each day. When the gifts are offered by the priest, he says: "Blessed are you, Lord God of all creation, for through your goodness we have received the bread we offer you: fruit of the earth and work of human hands..." And in offering the cup he says" "Blessed are you, Lord, God of all creation, for through your goodness we have received the wine we offer you: fruit of the vine and work of human hands..." And just before receiving Communion himself, the priest prays: "Lord Jesus Christ, Son of the living God, who by the will of the Father and the work of the Holy Spirit, through your death gave life to the world..."

The "work of human hands" produces the bread and wine that become the body and blood of Christ. By the "work of the Holy Spirit"

Christ's death brought life to the world. God is always at work in our world so that we might live. Moreover, God chooses to do his work in the world through the likes of us!

Every Monday, at the beginning of the workweek, the Church in its official "Daytime Prayer," familiar to all who recite the liturgy of the hours, prays: "God our Father, work is your gift to us, a call to reach new heights by using our talents for the good of all. Guide us as we work and teach us to live in the spirit that has made us your sons and daughters, in the love that has made us brothers and sisters."

"Work is your gift to us." That refers to the work you do each day or the employment from which you may have retired only to be free to do work of other kinds—volunteer work, charitable work, service to others. And in a special way, the phrase "work is your gift to us" refers to the work you initiates are undertaking now by way of preparation for baptism and full communion with the Church. You are so extraordinarily gifted with the grace of God that brings you to this moment. You and all the rest of us are gifted with talents that enable us to work with and for one another "in the spirit that has made us [God's] sons and daughters, in the love that has made us brothers and sisters."

It isn't always that way in the nine-to-five, Monday-through-Friday workplace, we know, but we should try to make it so. I can't tell you how often I've recalled, since the terrorist attacks of September 11, 2001, a remark made by Rabbi Abraham Joshua Heschel just around the time the Twin Towers of the World Trade Center were built in the 1970s. "Our concern," he said, "is not with how to worship in the catacombs; our concern is how to remain human in the skyscrapers." That is still our concern—how to remain human in the skyscrapers or wherever else we work each day. God is there in your work. Others can see God in you at work, if you bring to the workplace "the love that has made us brothers and sisters."

The first encyclical letter written by Pope John Paul II was "On Human Work." He stressed the dignity of human labor, the right of workers to organize in order to gain and protect their rights, and he used the metaphor of the great "workbench" where every man and woman seeking work had a right, by virtue of their human dignity, to find a place, and at that place, to use their talents for the development of their own human potential and for the good of the human community.

St. Paul addressed a disorder in the Christian community at Thessalonica where some were "unwilling to work...conducting themselves...in a disorderly way, by not keeping busy but minding the business of others." If they refused to work, he said, they should not eat. And then he instructed all "to work quietly and to eat their own food."

Let me suggest a parallel between work and communion, a joining-at-the-hip, so to speak of the workbench and the altar viewed as a Communion table. You who participate in these rites of initiation that begin today will soon be approaching the Table of the Lord. You also have some place somewhere at the workbench of daily life. Make yourselves aware of the link between the two. Let your offertory procession begin each Monday at the workbench, and carry from there through the week the work of human hands. Carry it to the altar on Sunday along with gifts of bread and wine that will be offered by you to God, who will return the bread and wine to you as the body and blood of his Son, and will return your works with his blessing for your good and the good of all the world. Then you will return on Monday—refreshed, strengthened, and renewed—from the altar, where you ate your special food, to the workbench, where you can continue to pursue, by God's grace, the work of human hands.

67

Thirty-Fourth or Last Sunday of the Year, Solemnity of Our Lord Jesus Christ, King Of the Universe

The Good Thief

2 Samuel 5:1–3; Psalm 122; Colossians 1:12–20; Luke 23:35–43

It is interesting that today, on the Solemnity of Christ the King, the Church invites you to reflect on the Gospel story of the Good Thief. Tradition identifies him by the name of Dismas. Devotion honors him by calling him St. Dismas, a patron of criminals, prisoners, and particularly thieves.

His words have found their way into the haunting psalm-like hymn sung by the monks of Taizé in France: "Jesus, remember me, when you come into your kingdom; Jesus, remember me when you come into your kingdom." So there it is, the relationship between the thief, the Good Thief, and Christ the King, the ruler of a kingdom. And here we are—thieves to one degree or another, sinners all—facing Christ today in both celebration of his kingship and acknowledgment of our dependence upon him for safe conduct through this world and on into eternal life.

"Jesus, remember me, when you come into your kingdom; Jesus, remember me, when you come into your kingdom."

I always think of Cardinal Joseph Bernardin when I hear those words, especially in the melodic form of the Taizé rendition, famous for its calming repetition. The words were sung at the end of Cardinal Bernardin's funeral liturgy in Holy Name Cathedral in Chicago in November 1996, as his body was brought down the aisle and out to an awaiting hearse on the street. Over and over again, people in the crowded cathedral and on the street outside softly sang, "Jesus, remember me, when you come into your kingdom; Jesus, remember me, when you come into your kingdom."

239

In the Gospel story you just heard from Luke 23, Jesus responds to that request in words that each one of us surely hopes to hear: "today you will be with me in Paradise." You will hear that response if your request comes from a sincere and repentant heart, from an honest acknowledgment of both the power of Jesus to save and your need for salvation, just as Dismas, the Good Thief, declared his faith and his need from his position on a cross next to the cross of Christ.

You will recall that there were two thieves crucified along with Christ, one on either side. As Luke paints the picture for you, "One of the criminals hanging there reviled Jesus, saying, 'Are you not the Messiah? Save yourself and us.'" But the other thief, the so-called Good Thief, rebuked him: "Have you no fear of God, for you are subject to the same condemnation? And indeed, we have been condemned justly, for the sentence we received corresponds to our crimes, but this man has done nothing criminal." And with that, this crucified thief turns and says, "Jesus, remember me when you come into your kingdom." His request was made; his prayer was heard.

There's a maximum security prison in Dannemora, in upstate New York, that has a church within the walls; it is called the "Church of the Good Thief," built by inmate labor in the late 1930s. The Catholic chaplain at that time, Fr. Ambrose Hyland, came up with the idea of providing worship space for prisoners and using the project as an occasion to teach building construction skills to inmates, including specialized skills like making stained glass windows. That structure still stands and is in service to the inmate population.

In St. Louis in the 1950s, there was a famous Jesuit priest named Charlie Clark who ministered to inmates in the city jail and followed them on to the large state prison in Jefferson City, Missouri. He was so committed to ministry to criminals that he took the name "Dismas" and was known as "The Hoodlum Priest." As a Jesuit seminarian studying at St. Louis University, I once went to St. John's Hospital to donate blood for the then dying Jesuit Fr. Daniel Lord. There was a rather tough looking construction worker in the waiting room where I, dressed in my roman collar, was sitting. This fellow was also there to donate blood. He looked straight at me and asked, "Do you know Fr. Clark?" Before I could acknowledge that I did, this man, who may have served jail time himself, said, "I know a lot of guys who would gladly go to the chair for Fr. Clark."

One of the death-row inmates in Jefferson City who was being helped by Fr. Clark, told him that he wanted to paint a picture of St. Dismas and asked what he looked like. Fr. Clark told him he should try to get all the good and evil he could imagine into one face and that would serve as an accurate representation of the Good Thief. I was with Fr. Clark in his room at the old Queen's Work Jesuit residence when he told me this story and there, in the corner of the room, was the painting—a floor-to-ceiling representation of Dismas on the cross. The face was interesting. From the bridge of the nose to the top of the head it was a representation of Fr. Clark; from the bridge of the nose down to the chin, it was the inmate himself. One man's idea of a combination of good and evil; one man's expression of devotion to Dismas and admiration for Fr. Clark.

The second reading in today's liturgy, the selection from the Letter to the Colossians, urges you to give "thanks to the Father, who has made you fit to share in the inheritance of the holy ones in light. He delivered us from the power of darkness and transferred us to the kingdom of his beloved son."

Well, this is what happened to Dismas, the Good Thief; he was rescued there on Calvary, where darkness had descended on the world, and he was admitted directly to the kingdom. This is also what awaits each one of you who prays today, on the Solemnity of Christ the King, in the words of the Good Thief, saying: "Jesus, remember me, when you come into your kingdom." Well, Jesus is there now, in that kingdom and will be king forever. He does and will indeed remember you. Through him, the letter to the Colossians tells us, "we have redemption, the forgiveness of sins."

Say it in the words of Dismas or words of your own. Sing it as it is sung by the monks of Taizé. Or whisper the request in your own quiet prayer. Just say it: "Jesus, remember me when you come into your kingdom." He is reigning now; he is Christ your king. And he responds to you as he responded to the Good thief: "today you will be with me in paradise."